EXCEL VBA

---◆●◆---

THE ULTIMATE INTERMEDIATE'S GUIDE TO LEARN VBA PROGRAMMING STEP BY STEP

David A. Williams

Table Of Contents

Introduction 4

VBA Integrated Development Environment 9

Control Program Flow and Making Decisions in Visual Basic for Application 18

How to Avoid Common Mistakes in Excel VBA 33

Interacting with the user 40

The "Speed Search Control Panel And Timing Comparison" Application 56

Performing Statistical Analysis Using Formulas 67

Scenario Building with One-way Data Table 83

An Event Macro 98

The Macro Recorder 110

The Excel Object Model 127

Derived Data Types in VBA 137

Beyond the Basics 141

The Cheat Sheet for Excel Formulas 146

Some other tips on VBA programming 151

Search And Reference Formulas 163

Department Data Validation 169

The Object Model 180

Relative and Absolute References 187

Project – Registration Form 201
A Sample Program 222
More Examples 244
Conclusion 251

INTRODUCTION

Excel is the most popular spreadsheet software in the world today. It was developed by the giant software company Microsoft Inc. and is the single most widely used spreadsheet program in businesses, government, schools, universities, and other institutions.

While there are many different spreadsheet programs available, Excel remains number one. It has continued to enjoy widespread use and massive growth over the past three decades. There have been numerous upgrades and new features introduced over the years.

Excel finds application in many different fields, including business intelligence, finance, statistics, analysis, forecasting, billing, inventory, data management, and so much more. This is why numerous employees and workers are required to learn how to use this application if they are to be effective in the workplace.

Most employers view Excel as an essential end-user computing tool, especially those in the fields of accounting, information systems, and business in general. It is widely used to carry out daily functions at the workplace.

The first thing to check when preparing to use VBA for Excel is whether macros have been enabled in the Excel version being used. To do this, go to the developer option on the toolbar and click on Macro Security and enable the usage of Macros.

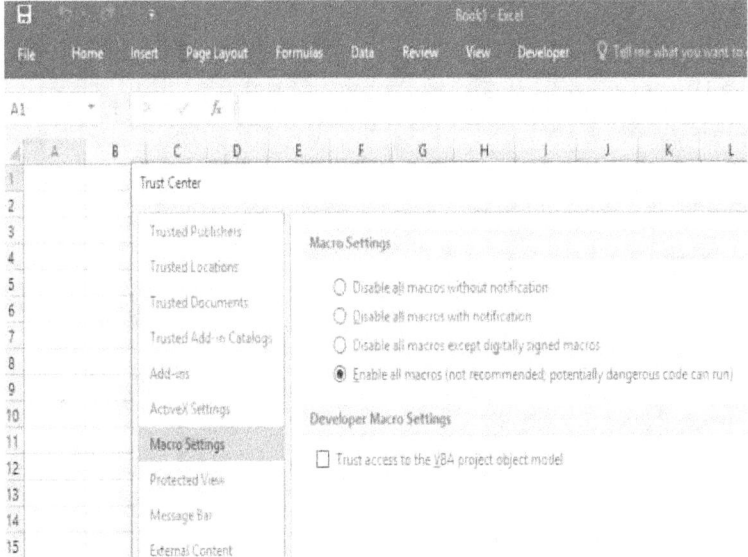

Notice the above screenshot is for Excel 2016. This feature can be turned off after practicing the parts of this book.

Now that the macros are enabled to get familiar with when programming with Excel is the Visual Basic Interface/ Editor.

This can be opened in Excel 2016 by again clicking on the Developer option on the main toolbar and choosing Visual Basic on the extreme left corner.

Clicking this option will lead to the following screen/editor, as shown in the picture below.

The white area on the right will become visible when clicking on sheet one on the left-hand side. This is the default level, and many sheets can be created depending on the project.

In this screen, the code for each sheet and object on the sheet will be written on the right-hand side white area.

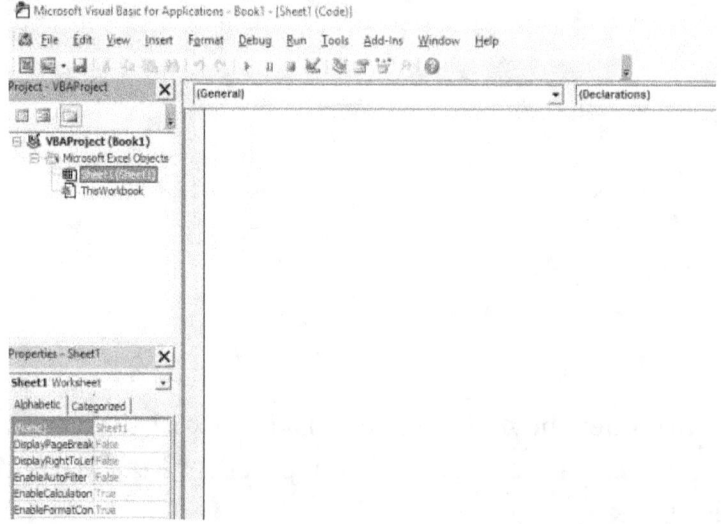

The various properties of the sheet and of objects will be shown on the lower left. This is similar to that in Visual Basic.

One can select the properties and give it values through this segment of the editor; however, the same can be done in code. The more professional way is the latter.

On the top of the toolbar, the features that are needed the most are debugged and run. Run makes the code run if every line of code is okay. Keep in mind that logical errors are not checked by the debugger.

On running the code, a name for the new macro will be requested. Enter the first macro for now and hit create. This macro will be a blank macro as no code has been added to it.

A subroutine called the first macro will be created on the right-hand side of the editor as follows.

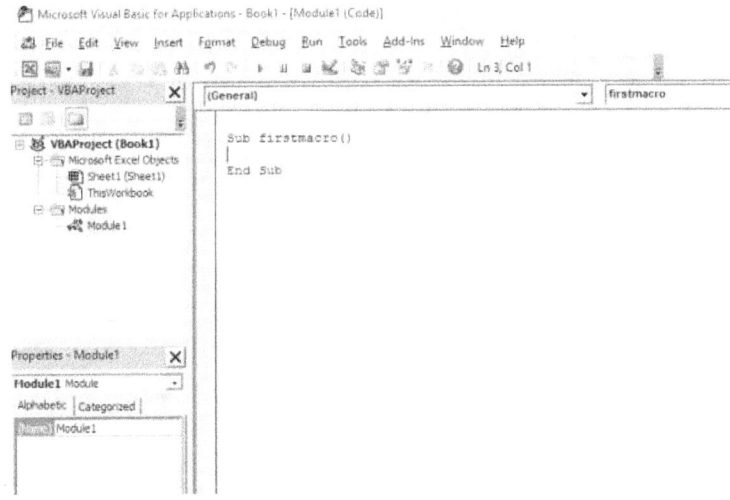

Note that module1 has been added to the left-hand side of the editor's top and bottom.

To display the words "Hello World" write the following on the right-hand side within the subroutine first macro as follows:

    Sub firstmacro()

Msgbox("Hello World")

End Sub

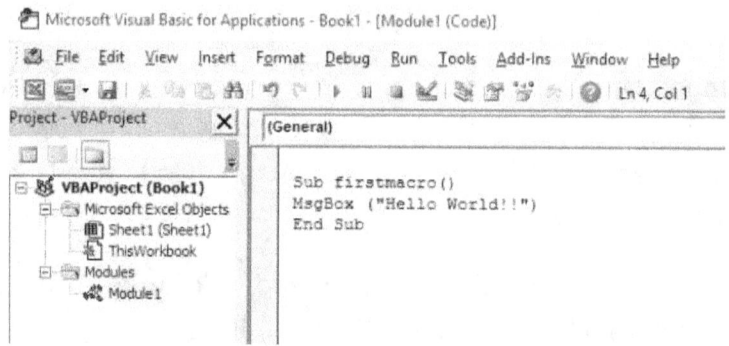

Now run the program using the green > arrow on the top of the code on the sub toolbar or the run option on the toolbar. The following will be the result.

This is the starting point of writing VBA. The steps that have been done so far will be repeated again and again in the parts that follow.

VBA INTEGRATED DEVELOPMENT ENVIRONMENT

Getting into IDE

The Visual Basic Applications for computer programs are consolidated inside all parts of the Microsoft Office suite for projects like Excel. Initiating the VBA advancement programming sets the programming condition for the IDE, which allows tools for use in working up the venture. The speediest way into the VBA IDE is to click on Alt+F11 within the essential Excel window.

It is similarly possible to confer from the standard Excel menu through tools, at that point, Macro and afterward, the Visual Basic Editor. In the wake of initiating the IDE, a window for the outlining of the VBA IDE and a segment of the tools utilized for the production of projects will be created. In numerous applications, there happens to be a menu bar over the highest point of the window. You may simply see a few things that exist inside the menu, and these will become evident as you proceed through the manuscript.

One of the essential things would be the explorer window as showed up on the topmost left area of the

IDE window. The toolbar explorer records the projects that are right by and by open, including the ones accessed via Excel amidst the startup.

Besides that, the endeavor explorer records parts of any of the accessed projects in the running with the figure; there is an outline of one envisions known as Book 1. In the wake of opening it, it contains four Excel objects that are sheet 1, 2, 3, and this workbook 1.

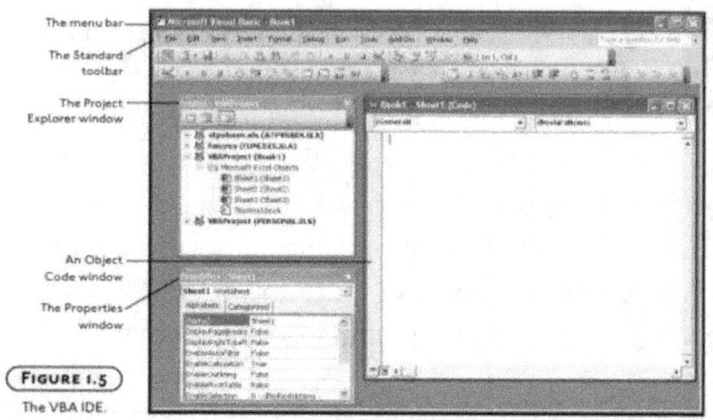

FIGURE 1.5 The VBA IDE.

Just under the venture explorer window, as showed up in the above figure, refers to the properties setting. The latter shows a quick overview of the highlights or elements of the fundamental object found in the project. These characteristics are needed to control the manifestation of the question where they have a place.

The elements of sheet 1 appear in the above figure as picked inside the undertaking explorer. Confirmation of some other object will allow understanding of a properties list inside the properties window. Few parts of the objects have relative properties. The main thing inside the control of properties is to open another workbook and set the names.

In the event the undertaking explorer and the properties windows are not starting at now demonstrated, then one can get to them by techniques for the view menu. You may also use the keystrokes F4 and CTRL + R with a specific target to get to the undertaking explorer and properties windows. At the time that the undertaking explorer window is displayed, discover the venture, which is illustrative of the workbook opened while in Excel. If the workbook portions opened are not set, then click the + sign, which is close by Microsoft Excel objects organizer that is under the undertaking name.

Then, consider the object that is named sheet one and a short time after selecting it by then look towards the properties window. The subsequent stage would be to consider down the properties window until the point, and one would arrive at Name property, which is the one without the segment.

You can go to Excel by clicking Alt + F11 from the taskbar. It will be evident the name of the sheet has, at present, been supplanted with MySheet inside the Excel workbook. It has each one of the stores of being unquestionably not hard to change the properties of the worksheet in Excel with the utilization of VBA. As the VBA is creative, it will not be hard to change the properties of the worksheet or workbook at the set time. By far, most of the work affects the worksheets, and the workbooks would occur during the runtime, as the goal is to alter the properties of ActiveX controls.

In the event, one considers the figure of now; there is a standard window. These are used as compartments for the projects. It is placed within the program's coding, so these windows function as content directors that take after Notepad. As the client, one has to understand there exist pre-portrayed code windows, particularly for Excel items, for example, the workbook.

The code window that displayed in the figure addressed starting at now exhibits sheet one that is contained in the workbook known as Book 1. There are more parts to the VBA IDE, though this is sufficient information to begin with. Depending on the necessity, there will be further explanation of other functionalities within the IDE leading furthering of projects.

Programming parts in Excel

Not every attractive element of the VBA programming software is located inside the VBA IDE. Some programming-related parts are those that one can obtain from Excel. The parts in this setting join the larger scale of items that are detailed within the menu for the tools, and three of the toolbars, Visual Basic, and the toolbox is placed inside Excel's in-view menu.

Since the presentation part of VBA IDE has been anchored, it is pertinent to consider how tools got can be arranged from Excel. Consider the vast scale choice from the tools menu illustrated in the running. You should also note the different items that displayed up in the figure, which have not yet been tied down for these future Macros and Recording of new macros.

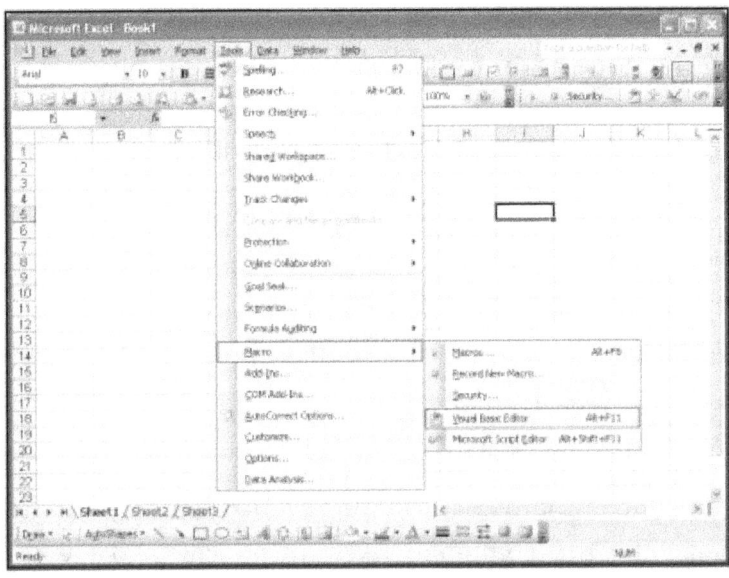

The tool allows the customer to make a VBA program by demonstrating a box set with a claim for most of the VBA software that has been illustrated. The item along these lines is a way to deal with access and run of required VBA programs. Macros generally insinuate the projects recorded while the customer performs a movement of errands in the common application interface.

Their use comes in when the customer more than once does errands in Excel in the same way. Rather than reiterating the assignments, the customer may record their exercises and then playback the full scale when they need to go over a similar game plan. It is possible anyway for one to get to the projects that had not been recorded through the large-scale menu object.

The Visual Basic toolbar gives a game plan of tools to the VBA designer. As officially indicated, picking the crucial visual editor from the settings is going to allow for access. There are other basics illustrated in the Visual Basic setting.

They include the Record Macro, Design Mode, and Run Macro. Similarly included concerning the Visual Basic would be the icon for the control toolbox. The control toolbox may also be gotten to through the toolbars things that are on the view menu.

The control toolbox gives one ActiveX controls that are tools like the command button and checkbox, which could be connected with a vast scale. The command button, content box, and picture control are a bit of the ActiveX controls that are there. You can first tie the controls on a worksheet by clicking the pined for control and after that drawing in it to the worksheet. After the command button has been set out to the worksheet, you will find that it is picked, and the application is started within the outline mode. You may get to the elements of the command button settings while in plan mode.

Then you may go to the icon for properties. One like properties window in VBA IDE comes up. This illustrates many of the features utilized as a means of depicting the command button control.

The properties window at this time records an extensive segment of the features or properties that have been used as a touch of depicting the command button control. Concerning the button's control properties setting of the command, it is possible to manipulate the scratching characteristic to click and depict how the new subtitle shows up on the controls. Similarly, you may manipulate the Name property to another, for instance, cmdColorChange.

The prefix cmd for this condition references the kind of control (command button) while whatever is left of the name is a reference to parts of the program, which are begun at the time that the button is pressed. One may similarly play with a segment of trade properties like the text style, back-color, forecolor, and the stature recalling the real objective to tinker with the closeness of the control.

It is even possible to show a photograph inside the command button setting through the property then consider a photo narrative from the PC.

At the time, the command control button is done, select, from the control toolbox, the view code flip, or select the command button with a particular focus to get to the window for the code. This will lead you to the VBA IDE. Then manipulate the command to embed. The best way is to deal with oversight for this is adding code to the code window. The title bar clearly outlines on the request, which the code window has located. Here, the code window has a link with the worksheet, which is known as sheet one inside the workbook named book 1.

In the top left setting of the code, the window shows a drop-down rundown box that has a compartment with the names of the objects that are in the worksheet selected. The command button's name is then shown, considering the cursor is in the editor that has an approach of the command. The running with the figure demonstrates the IDE with the code window.

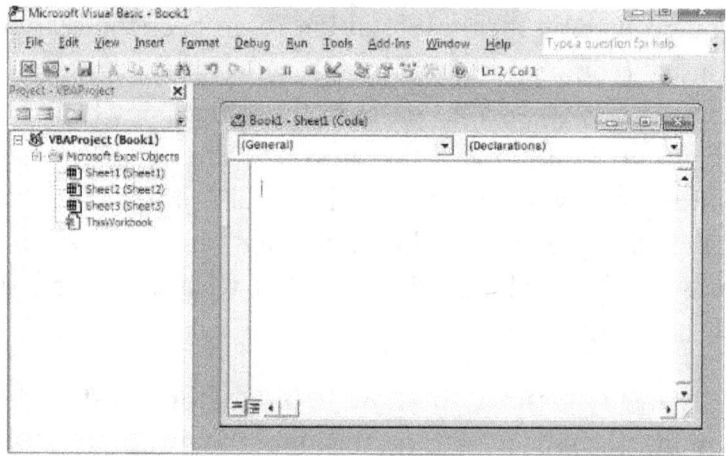

The procedures for events are earlier characterized as are controls of ActiveX and other objects inside the Excel scope. These protocols for the object chosen are recorded inside the top right placing of the window within a run-down box. The click event is basic as the protocol with a number of the ActiveX controls. Any of the codes that are arranged inside the predefined procedure would end up triggering at the time the client taps the object. In this circumstance, that would be the command button control, which is assigned CMDcolorchange. The name of this process would be the object's name underscored then took after by the name of the event.

It isn't possible to change the name of the pre-characterized occasion process without changing the name property for the object. On the off chance that you distort the name of the process, the code inside the process wouldn't keep running at the time it is required.

The keyword Sub is required and would be utilized as an originator for the process, which is either software-engineer-characterized or event-oriented. The second line end Sub is, for the most part, utilized as a part of a request to close the process. In a case, writing out the inside the occasion procedure of the command button control is cmdColorChange.

Range("A1").Select.Cells.Interior.ColorIndex = Int(Rnd * 56) + 1

The shade for the cells is then used at random, at which point it would change according to the command frame as the code runs once each click.

CONTROL PROGRAM FLOW AND MAKING DECISIONS IN VISUAL BASIC FOR APPLICATION

Programming flow and making decisions are programming constructs that are used in the code when constructing it. There are multiple constructions such as GoTo statements, If-Then statements, Select-Case statements, For-Next loop, and Do-While/Do-Until loops.

Control structures allow the user to regulate the flow of the program execution, make decisions, and repeat some actions until a criterion is met.

Decision Structures

Decision structures are structures the allow the user to test conditions and perform different operations based on the result of the condition.

If-Then – Else Construction

It evaluates a condition and runs one or more statements based on the evaluation of the condition.

Example:

Dim number As Byte

If number > 10 then

    MsgBox "Number is greater than 10."

Else

    MsgBox "Number is less or equal with 10."

End if

Select – Case Construction

It evaluates a condition that can return more values and run one or more statements based on the result of the evaluation of the condition. This construction can also be written as multiple if-else constructions with the same result.

Example:

    Dim number As Byte

    Select Case number

        Case Is >=100

            MsgBox "High number."

        Case Is >=50

            MsgBox "Medium number."

        Case Is >=0

MsgBox "Low number."

Case Else

MsgBox "Something Wrong"

End Select

Try – Catch – Finally Construction

This type of construction lets the user run a set of statements under an environment that retains control if any of the other statements causes an error/exception. This construction evaluates a statement, and if it returns an error, it can prevent any errors in the code execution (error handling).

Example:

Dim n1,n2,n3 As Long

Try

n1 = n2 / n3 'this can through an error "Divide by Zero"

MsgBox "Result is : " & n1

Catch ex As Exception

MsgBox "Exception : " & ex

Finally

MsgBox "Operation executed"

End Try

Loop Structures

While Loops

This type of construction runs one or more statements as long the condition specified in the While statement is true (it is possible that the statements are not executed if the condition is not true). When this type of construction is used, make sure that the condition became true at one point; otherwise, the code will enter an infinite loop and crashes.

Example:

    Dim number As Byte

    Number = 0

    While number < 10

        MsgBox number

        number = number + 1 'variable will become ten and exit the

        while statement

    End While

Do Loops

This type of construction runs one or more statements as long the condition specified in the Until statement is true (for Do-While construction, statements will be run at least once even if the condition is false, as the condition is tested at the end). When this type of construction is used, make sure that the condition became true at one point; otherwise, the code will enter an infinite loop and crashes.

Example1:

    Dim number as Byte

    number = 0

    Do

        MsgBox number

        Number = number + 1

    While (number < 10)

Example2:

    Dim number As Byte

    Number = 0

    Do While (number < 10)

        MsgBox number

    Number = number + 1

Loop

For Loops

This type of construction initiates a variable with initial value and last value. The code runs the statements from the initial value until the last value of the variable and auto increment it.

Definition:

>For counter = start To end [Step]
>
>>[statements]
>
>[Continue For]
>
>>[statements]
>
>[Exit For]
>
>>[statements]
>
>Next [counter]

If it is needed to break the for and exit from it, it can be included an IF-Then structure inside the for and use "Exit For" syntax to exit the for loop at any time. For structures are the easiest way to loop through an array items.

Next syntax (last line for the for construction), it auto-increment the value with the specified step (positive or negative step).

Example1:

>Dim number As Byte
>
>For number = 0 to 10
>
>>MsgBox number

Next number

-numbers from 0 to 10 will be displayed ascending

Example2:

Dim number As Byte

For number = 10 to 0 Step -1

MsgBox number

Next number

-numbers from 10 to 0 will be displayed descending

Example3:

Dim Names(10) As String

Dim i as Byte

Names(0) = "ABC"

Names(1) = "BCD"

Names(2) = "CDE"

Names(3) = "DEF"

Names(4) = "EFG"

Names(5) = "FGH"

Names(6) = "GHI"

Names(7) = "HIJ"

Names(8) = "IJK"

Names(9) = "JKL"

For i = 0 to 9

    If Names(i) = "FGH" then

        MsgBox "FGH reached. For will be exit."

Exit For

    Else

    MsgBox Names(i)

End If

Next i

The for construction will loop through Names array and display the names from the array. If the name is equal with "FGH," then the for construction will be interrupted (exit for)

For Each Loop

This type of construction is similar to for-next construction, and the only difference is that this construction is used to loop through elements of an array or list without an index (it loops through values directly). The code runs the statements from the first value until the last value of the structure and auto-increment.

Definition:

    For Each element In group

        [statements]

    [Continue For]

        [statements]

    [Exit For]

        [statements]

    Next [element]

Example1:

Dim listOfNames as New List(of String) From_ ("ABC","BCD","CDE","DEF")

    For Each item As String In listOfNames

        MsgBox item

    Next

Example2:

    Dim numbers(3) as Byte = (1,2,3)

    Dim nr as Byte

    Dim letters(3) As Char = {"a", "b", "c"}

    Dim lett as Char

    For Each nr in numbers

>   For Each lett in letters
>
>   MsgBox nr & " " & lett
>
>   Next
>
> Next

This example loops through both list (numbers and letters) and will display the combination of the items (1a; 2a; 3a; 1b; 2b; 3b; etc.)

Other Control Structures

Using – End Structure

This structure construction establishes a statement block within the user can use a resource (example SQL connection – needs to close all SQL connections after interrogation of a database). The resource can be acquired with Using keyword (when inserting Using keyword VBA will automatically display a list of possible resources that can be used).

Definition:

> Using { resourceList | resourceExpression }
>
>   [statements]
>
> End Using

Example:

Sub WriteToTXTFile()

```vb
Using writer As System.IO.TextWriter = _
System.IO.File.CreateText("filename.txt")

    writer.WriteLine("First line of text.")

    writer.WriteLine("Second line of text.")

    writer.WriteLine("Third line of text.")

End Using

End Sub

Sub ReadFromTXTFile()

Using reader As System.IO.TextReader = _
System.IO.File.OpenText("filename.txt")

    Dim lineText As String

        lineText = reader.ReadLine()

    Do Until line Is Nothing

        MsgBox lineText

        lineText = reader.ReadLine()

    Loop

End Using

End Sub
```

In this example are created two subs, one to create a txt file (filename.txt) and write 3 lines inside the file, and the second one is to read the content of the txt file and message line by line the content of the file. Because of the TextWriter and TextReader classes implement in the IDisposable interface the code use Using keyword to ensure that the txt file is closed right after read/write operations.

With – End Structure

This structure allows the user to specify an object reference once and then access its members. This structure improves performance of the code because the Visual Basic does not have to establish the reference for each member, it establishes the reference once and access multiple members of it.

Definition:

    With objectExpression

        [statements]

    End With

Example1:

    With Application

        Calculation = xlCalculationAutomatic

        ScreenUpdating = True

        DisplayAlerts = True

        EnableEvents = True

    End With

This example set some application properties (used to improve the speed and performance of the code) by establishing the reference for Application just once and modify four of the members (without this structure it is needed to create four Application references which slows down the code)

Example2:

With ThisWorkbook.Sheets(1).Range("A1:A1")

    .Value = 2

    .BackgroundColor = RGB (0,0,255)

    .Borders(xlEdgeBottom).LineStyle = xlContinuous

End With

this example set value, background color and border for a cell by establishing the reference to Range property only once (establish reference once, modify 3 parameters)

Nested Control Structures

It refers to the possibility of combine multiple structures, some control statements inside other control statements.

Nesting Levels

All the control structures can be nested as many times is needed and as many levels as are needed.

Example:

>Dim i, j As Long
>
>For i = 1 to 100
>
>>For j = 1 to 100
>>
>>>If i < j then
>>>
>>>>'Statements
>>>
>>>Else
>>>
>>>>'Statements
>>>
>>>End If
>>
>>Next
>
>Next

Nesting Different Kinds of Control Structures

Different types of controls can be nested together.

Example:

>Dim i, j As Long
>
>For i = 1 to 100
>
>>j = i
>>
>>While j < 50
>>
>>>If i + j < 100 then

                'Statements

           Else

                'Statements

           End If

           j = j +1

      Next

  Next

Overlapping Control Structures

Control structures can also be overlapped (ex. while structure can overlap for structure).

HOW TO AVOID COMMON MISTAKES IN EXCEL VBA

There is a lot to learn in Excel VBA and it can easily overwhelm you if you're not careful. As a beginner, you may find that you will make more mistakes than you would like to. Don't worry about that, it is perfectly normal however, there are a few tricks that can help you from venturing off down the wrong path so you don't have to back track and fix them.

It is true that we all learn from our mistakes but especially in the world of business, mistakes can quite often prove costly. Learning how to use VBA is like learning any other skill, which means that there is only so much you can learn from a book, the rest must be acquired through practice. Remember, nothing worth learning can be glossed over and rushed. So take your time and practice these skills over and over again until they feel like second nature to you. If you take the time to do this first, before you expose your newfound skill to your business, you'll have less chance of making those kinds of errors that could prove costly.

Still, there are a number of common mistakes people make with VBA that are definitely worth taking a closer look at. By being aware of these types of mistakes you can use your practice sessions to figure out ways to work around them so you are less likely to fall into those traps when you take your new skills and apply them in real life.

Overusing Select and Activate

Select and Activate are two of the most common commands you use when using a macro recorder. However, more often than not they are not even necessary. In many cases, using them could prove to be quite redundant for several reasons. So, if you don't need this particular function then it's a better idea to delete those commands altogether. Once you do, you will see the code improve, working faster than normal. However, if you feel you will need to perform either of these two functions, it is a good idea to keep the commands in place as it is a means of ensuring the code continues to function in the correct way.

Overuse of the variant type

Sometimes new users of VBA can get the many variant types confused. You may think that you are using one type when in actuality you are using a totally different one. For example, using a Dim code such as "Dim d, e, f as Long". You might assume that this is a Long type variant. It's a logical conclusion and a mistake that many newbies actually make.

If you've made this mistake, don't worry, you're in good company. However, only types "d", and "e" would be variant types, meaning that they can be any type and can be changed from one type to the other whenever needed.

Using this type of coding can be very tricky and confusing. Since using them could create a lot of errors in the code that could be extremely difficult to find. Because this is such an easy mistake to make, it may be a good idea to avoid using Variant variables in the beginning. Once you become more familiar with the other more basic forms of coding you can gradually ease your head into the lion's mouth and practice this more advanced form. It will save you a lot of problems that will inevitably cause you frustration if you do.

Underuse of the Application.ScreenUpdating = False

Every time you make a change to a cell in your worksheet, Excel will go through and update the screen. This will ensure that your new changes appear as you make them. If you are working for an extended amount of time, you could easily input a lot of data. Depending on the power of your computer and the amount of data you've accumulated, it could lead to a lag time in the system if it is not updated. To do this, you can always stop your work at some point and do an update by following the code below:

> Public Sub MakeCodeFaster()
>
> Application.ScreendUpdating = False
>
> 'do some stuff

'Always remember to reset this setting back!

Application.ScreenUpdating = True

End Sub

While the system does automatically update the screen periodically. If the data you're working with is very important, it never hurts to add a manual update to protect your work.

Adding a name of a worksheet to a string when it is not necessary

It can be very tempting to write codes referencing the specific name of a worksheet. It can be a means of ensuring that the program will access the correct worksheet in a string. However, when working in VBA this is not necessary. Consider this example:

Public Sub SheetReferenceExample()

Dim ws As Worksheet

Set ws = Sheets("Sheet1")

Debug.Print ws.Name

End Sub

While this type of mistake won't yield you any negative impact, if you do not break this habit, it may cause difficulties for others who try to use your programs. For example, if you took your worksheet and gave it to someone else who wanted to rename it, then it may no longer function as it should because you've named the worksheet when it wasn't necessary. So, in the interest of camaraderie, it just makes sense that you try not to develop this type of habit in the first place.

The best practice is to make sure that all of your references directly point to a corresponding object and then allow the program to find the sheet. As long as you have added the right code, you will see Sheet1 and not a series of sheets.

Failing to qualify range references

When working with VBA, beginners usually fail to qualify their range references. This is a common error as many newbies are not really sure what to look for. So, it is very important that you take extra care to ensure that you qualify all references as soon as possible so you don't get stalled after.

If you're unsure of either what a range reference is or you're in doubt about how to find them, here is are a few things to keep in mind that could help you.

If the code is Range (A1) then you need to consider the exact worksheet it is referring back to. Your answer to this problem will always refer to your active sheet unless there is something else in the code that is referencing a different page. As a rule of thumb, the ActiveSheet will always be the sheet that is currently under rechecking.

If you use Range() without specifying which worksheet to use, Excel will automatically assume that you are referencing the active sheet. So, if you want to reference a different sheet, you need to make sure that is added to your code beforehand.

Sub functions that are too long

If you create a function and the result is longer than a single page of your module then there is a good chance that it is too complicated or too long. Long codes are not a problem in and of themselves but the more complex the code is the more of a chance of error or of a code that lags and bogs down the system. There are quite a few things you can do to prevent your code from just going over the top. But one of the easiest ways to avoid this problem is to pay extra attention to keeping the Sub and Function methods as lean as possible. Make good use of any helper functions or any possible sub procedures you can apply that will help you to do this.

It is inevitable that you will make mistakes and you learn this new skill but those that take the time, practice, and pick up on these many tricks will master it much faster than many others who just enjoy the experience of diving right in.

We all know how complicated and confusing these things can be when you are just learning how to use Excel VBA. No doubt, it will take an investment in time to make sure you fully understand exactly how the module works and what you have to do. If by some chance, you are having issues with the coding, take the time to look up some of the more common problems that others face and learn how they fixed them.

INTERACTING WITH THE USER

Introduction

With VBA you can also make applications that look professional. So far we have worked with the fundamentals that will allow us to handle many of the strengths that make Excel and its programming language a very powerful tool for the development of applications. Now we will see how we can interact with the user of our applications, through forms (Userforms) that are no more than the windows in which requests for information are made or results are presented. The above can be done using either numbers, texts, images and / or graphics. VBA offers a wide variety of controls to display information to the user and to request it called widgets. Through these controls you can display information, show options for the user to choose, buttons that perform tasks, etc.

Userforms

Userforms are the main container which contains a graphical application. Within a form there will be labels, buttons, lists of options, text controls, etc. It is the interface with which the user interacts. Figure 11.1 shows how an empty form looks. It is composed of a main area where we will add our controls (enclosed in a rectangle). It has an "x" in the upper right corner, which allows closing the window (forever), which in turn terminates the execution of the program. This option is a "violent" way to exit the execution, since it is also a way to abort the execution of the program (or that portion of the program). In the upper left corner of the form there is a text that is often used to show the name of the application, but in general it can be customized with any message (in our figure it is where UserForm1 says).

Figure 11.2 shows a window with all the controls that can be added to a form to customize it. We will give a brief explanation of each of them, by building an application.

The application that we are going to develop is based on the subroutine 10.2 with the difference that now we will ask the user to enter the range of data that is taken into account for the calculations. The user can choose the calculation that he wants and the result will be shown in the form, instead of using the MsgBox function. Additionally, the program will count the number of samples in a range of ages.

In numeral 2.5 we showed how to add a form. To add a control, we select it from the Toolbox (figure 11.2) and drag it into the form. There we can move it to the position that we like and we can even change its size. Another way of adding a control is by clicking on it and moving the mouse to the form and clicking on it.

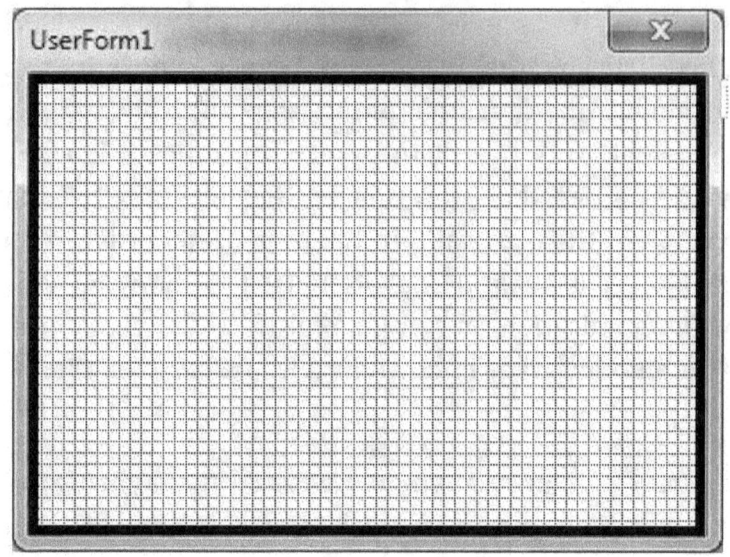

Userform.

Let's start by customizing our form. In figure 11.3 we can see it in the design phase. In case we want to modify the size we can do it by dragging one of the white squares that surround the form. It can also be done manually, modifying its Height and Width properties in the properties window (window located in the bottom left of figure 11.3).

Figure 11.2. Userform Toolbox (widgets).

The first thing we are going to do is change the name that the form will have. To do this, we change the Name property.. As can be seen in figure 11.3, the name (Name in the properties window) and the title (Caption) are the same. Changing the name does not change the title. The difference between both is that the name (Name) will be used to refer to the form in the code. The title can be a word or sentence that we want to show.

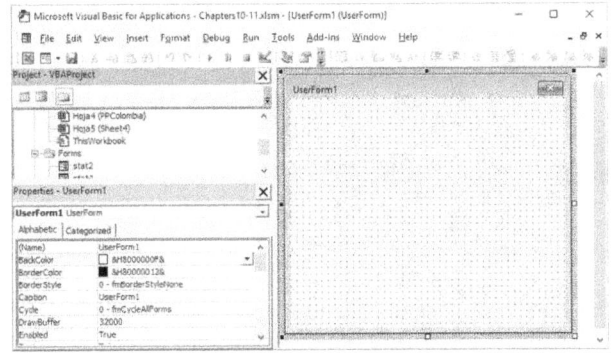

Figure 11.3. Form design phase.

The properties that we are going to change in the properties window are:

Property	Value
Name	Stat
Caption	Statistical software

We modify the size using the mouse.

Label

This control allows you to add a label with text that usually is not long. It is mostly used to give some information about another control or to show information to the user (which may vary as the application is running), such as a path to a file. The content of information in this control cannot be modified directly by the user at runtime, unless the modification is made from code.

For now we are going to add a label with information about the program. In figure 11.4 you can see what the message looks like and the properties that have been modified so far (enclosed in rectangles).

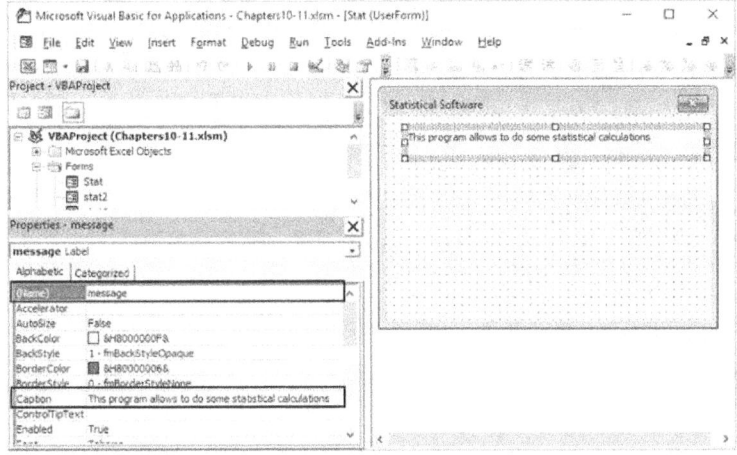

Figure 11.4. Label properties edition.

As we go adding other controls we will be adding more labels.

Figure 11.7. Adding checkboxes.

11.4 CommandButton

This button allows you to start the execution of a program. In its programming we have all the necessary code to make the calculations of our application. Although the execution of tasks is not exclusive of this control, it is what is most commonly practiced. You can also write code for events associated with other controls.

Figure 11.9 shows how our finally designed application looks now. It can also be noticed that we have added more labels, which are the ones that will show the results. These labels do not show text at the beginning of the execution. As the information they display may be of different sizes, you must change the AutoSize property of each label to True (as shown in figure 11.9) and the WordWrap property to False. Additionally we have added a button to close the application (Exit). We will program this button using the Click event.

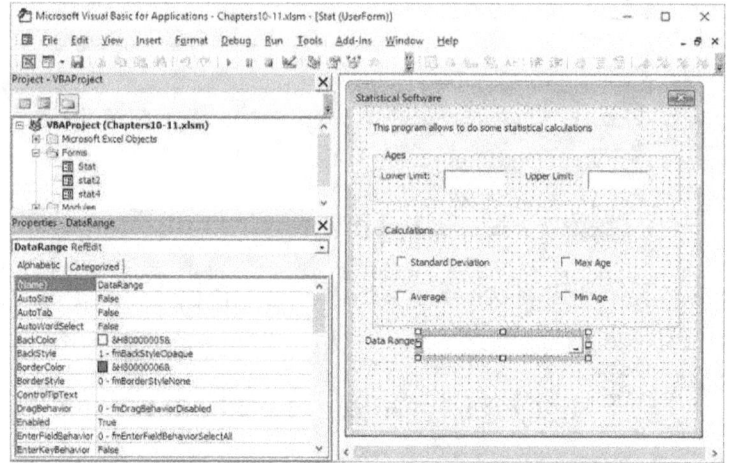

Figure 11.8. Adding Ref Edit widget.

To add the code that will be executed when you press the "Run" button, double-click on the button. This will automatically create the subroutine where the code will be contained (figure 11.10). By default, the subroutine that is created will be associated with the "Click" event. This means that the subroutine will be executed when the user makes a single click on the button. However, it is possible to associate another event.

In figure 11.10, inside the rectangle, two combo boxes can be observed. The one on the left contains all the controls that make up the application (figure 11.11).

The one on the right contains all the events that can be programmed for the control selected in the combo box on the left.

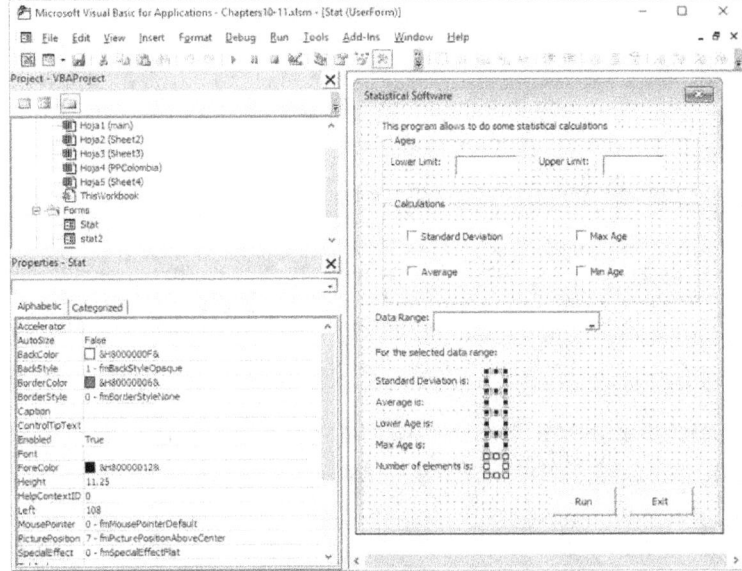

Figure 11.9. Adding command button and other labels.

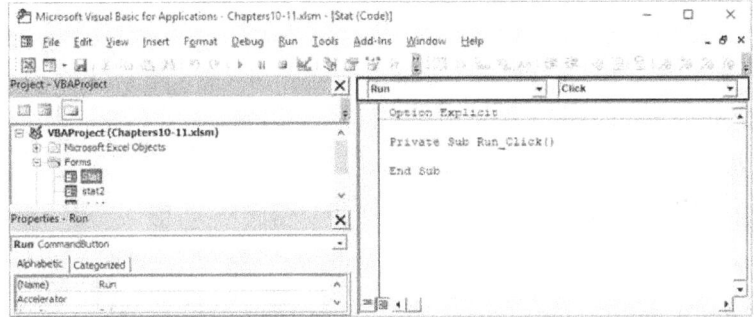

Figure 11.10. Window where the code of the "Run" button will be written.

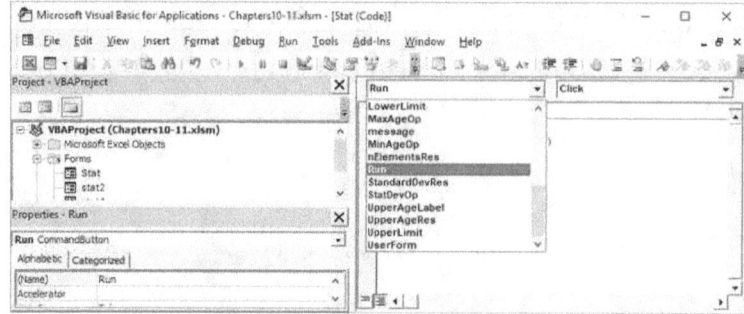

Figure 11.11. Controls that make up our application.

For example, in the case of the "Run" button, the possible events to program are those shown in figure 11.12.

Just to illustrate how events work, we will program our "Run" button to respond to the double-click of the mouse.

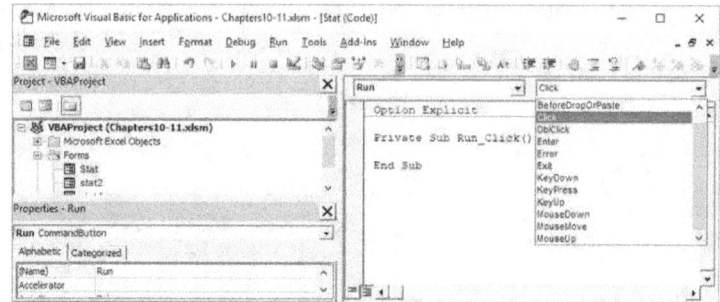

Figure 11.12. Events available for the "Run" button.

To add a subroutine associated with another event, select the event from the combo box on the right. Selecting the double-click event (DblClick) generates the space that will contain the subroutine, as shown in figure 11.13 (enclosed in the rectangle)

Figure 11.13. Space for the subroutine of the "Run" button associated with the Dblclick event.

We are also going to program the KeyPress event, which will be activated when the user, after clicking the "Run" button, now press any key. The program will show a message that this option is not valid to run the application. Figure 11.14 shows the body of the subroutine, associated with the KeyPress event (rectangle).

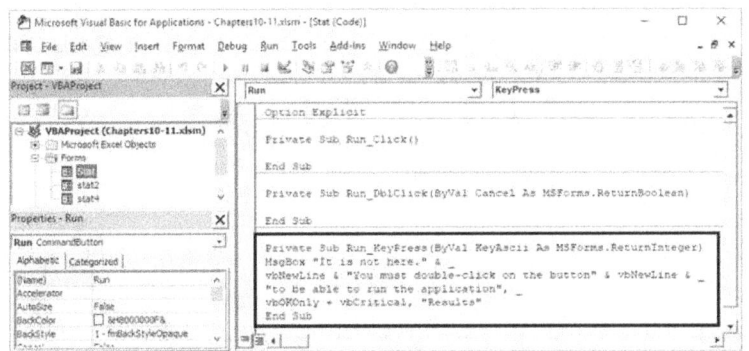

Figure 11.14. Subroutine for the KeyPress event of the "Run" button.

Subroutine 11.1 shows the code for the KeyPress event.

Subroutine 11.1.

1	Private Sub Run_KeyPress(ByVal KeyAscii As MSForms.ReturnInteger)
2	MsgBox "It is not here." & _
3	vbNewLine & "You must double-click on the button" & vbNewLine & _
4	"to be able to run the application", _
5	vbOKOnly + vbCritical, "Results"
6	End Sub

The subroutine 11.2 shows the code associated with the DblClick event of the "Run" button. This code is the one that will execute the calculations of the application.

Subroutine 11.2.

1	Private Sub Run_DblClick(ByVal Cancel As MSForms.ReturnBoolean)
2	Dim R As Range
3	Dim i, rows, n, lla, ula As Integer
4	
5	Set R = Range(DataRange.Value)

```vba
rows = R.rows.Count
n = 0
lla = CInt(LowerLimit.Value)    'Min Age
ula = CInt(UpperLimit.Value)    'Max Age

If lla >= WorksheetFunction.min(R) _
And ula <= WorksheetFunction.max(R) Then
    For i = 1 To rows + 1
        If R.Cells(i, 1).Value >= lla And _
           R.Cells(i, 1).Value <= ula Then
            n = n + 1
        End If
    Next i
End If

If StatDevOp.Value = True Then
```

22	StandardDevRes = VBA.Format(WorksheetFunction.StDev(R), "0.00")
23	End If
24	If AverageOp.Value = True Then
25	AverageRes = VBA.Format(WorksheetFunction.average(R), "0.00")
26	End If
27	If MinAgeOp.Value = True Then
28	LowerAgeRes = WorksheetFunction.min(R)
29	End If
30	If MaxAgeOp.Value = True Then
31	UpperAgeRes = WorksheetFunction.max(R)
32	End If
33	nElementsRes = n 'elements in the age range
34	End Sub

Some interesting comments about this code:

To select the range of cells, we place the mouse inside the DataRange control. Once there, we go to the spreadsheet and select the range of cells with the information we want to use as input.

That range of cells is read as a text string. In order to be used as a Range object, it is necessary to use the Range instruction (line 5). This range is assigned to the variable "R". Remember that in this case, the use of the reserved word Set is similar to use a nickname to make it easier and more practical to refer to the Range object.

In lines 8 and 9, we used the CInt instruction so that text strings read from text boxes are converted to numbers.

The checkboxes can only have two values: True or False (selected or not). This is what is evaluated in lines 21, 24, 27 and 30, for each of the four checkboxes used in the program.

To execute this program, you can press F5 or the button Execute macro (it is easy to recognize this button in the standard toolbar: it is a green triangle pointing to the right). This should be done in this way, since a form is not in itself a complete program, but part of a larger one. In order for an application with windows (forms) to be launched without having to be in the programming environment, its invocation must be done from (or be part of) a subroutine.

In figure 11.15 you can see a stage during the execution of the program, in which the selection of the range of cells to be used in the calculations is shown. Figure 11.16 shows the window with the results.

To exit the application, the "Exit" button was programmed. The code that is executed when pressing it is the one that is shown in subroutine 11.3.

Subroutine 11.3.

1	Private Sub ExitStat_Click()
2	Unload Me
3	End Sub

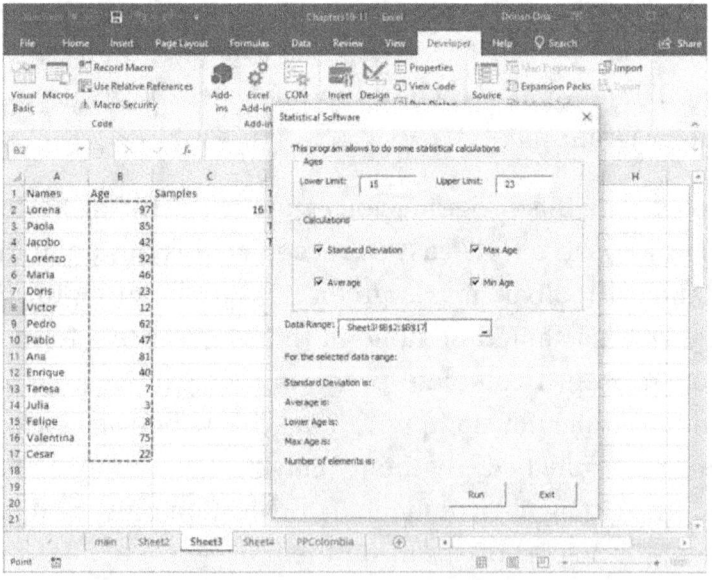

Figure 11.15. Running our application.

Interesting in this code is that the instruction to end the application refers to the object itself (Me). However, it can be changed by the name of the form: Stat. This means that the Unload statement can close any other form. Simply change the word Me for the name of the Userform (try changing Me by Stat on line 2).

THE "SPEED SEARCH CONTROL PANEL AND TIMING COMPARISON" APPLICATION

Please note that the run times will vary depending on your computer's processor and memory. The times shown below are based on an AMD Athlon II X2 250 Processor (3 GHz) and 6 GB of RAM. Intel I7 processors generally run a little slower than the AMD I used in my examples.

The VBA code within this control panel (which you can emulate in your own applications) illustrates techniques to search enormous ranges using various search methods and options to find EXACT matches. While some of the search methods are specifically designed by Microsoft to find only exact matches, the fastest search methods were designed to find either an exact match, or if one is not available, then find the closest match.

Since most applications require exact matches, the code in the control panel has been specifically modified to find ONLY exact matches, even for those methods that can find either and exact match or the closest match. All nine search methods produce identical results but with enormous run time differences.

The VBA code within the control panel demonstrates how to "program around" the limitations that are implicit in the native VLookup True and Match Option 1 commands. Here's a screen shot of the control panel application which you can download:

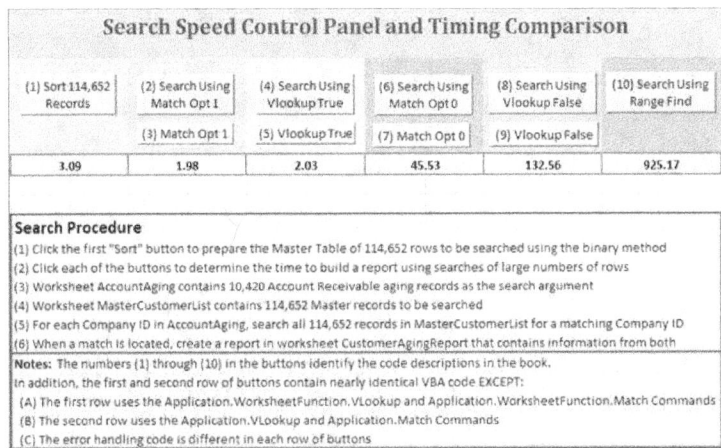

Notice that each button is identified by a number from 1 through 10. These numbers will be used to identify which button is being described below. For example, Button 2 is the "Search Using Match Opt 1". Button 3 is immediately below that button and is entitled "Match Opt 1". The odd numbered buttons (3, 5, 7, 9) refer to the lower of the button pairs.

Worksheets Used In The Control Panel Application

In the "Search Speed Control Panel and Timing Comparison" application there are four worksheets:

1) Worksheet "ControlPanel" includes a button to sort the range to be searched and nine other buttons that demonstrate different search methods and options. This worksheet also displays the resulting time it takes to run each search method to completion.

2) Worksheet "AccountAging" contains the following five columns used for Accounts Receivable aging.

Column Name	Contents
Company ID	The Company Identifier
30 Days	A/R > 0 Days, < 31 Days Due
60 Days	A/R > 30 Days, < 61 Days Due
90 Days	A/R > 60 Days, < 91 Days Due
Over 90 Days	A/R Over 90 Days Due

3) Worksheet "MasterCustomerList" contains the following twelve columns of information for each Company:

Column Name	Contents
Company ID	The Company Identifier
Company Name	Company Name
Address	Company Address

City	Company City
State	Company State
Zip	Company Zip
Contact First Name	Contact First Name
Contact Last Name	Contact Last Name
Phone 1	Company Phone 1
Phone 2	Company Phone 2
Email	Company Email
Web URL	Company Web URL

4) Worksheet "CustomerAgingReport" contains five columns of information composed of data collected from both the "AccountAging" and "MasterCustomerList" worksheets. When any of the buttons 2 through 10 are pressed, the entire contents of "CustomerAgingReport" are cleared and then rebuilt as the search procedures execute. The VLookup, Match and Range.Find methods are used to combine the information from worksheets "AccountAging" and "MasterCustomerList" and post the results to this worksheet, "CustomerAgingReport". The Company ID links the information in "AccountAging" and "MasterCustomerList".

Column Name	Contents
Company ID	The Company Identifier
Company Name	Company Name
90 Days	A/R > 60 Days, < 91 Days Due
Over 90 Days	A/R Over 90 Days Due
Phone 1	Company Phone 1

The Logic of the Search Speed Control Panel

The VBA code procedures in in the downloadable Speed Search Control Panel are good examples for you to incorporate into your own applications that require searches using the Match, VLookup or Range.Find methods.

For every one of the 10,420 rows in worksheet "AccountAging" (one row at a time) , the application uses the Company ID as a search argument to locate the matching Company ID in worksheet "MasterCustomerList". When a match is found, the company name and phone number from worksheet "MasterCustomerList" is used, along with data from "AccountAging" to create a report in worksheet "CustomerAgingReport". The master customer list contains 114,652 customers in ascending sequence.

That's a staggering 1.19 billion possible combinations to be searched.

The fastest method will allow this astonishing number of potential comparisons to be completed in just over 2 seconds (using my AMD processor). The slowest method (Range.Find) will require over 15 minutes and leave you wondering if your computer went to sleep.

In reality, the number of actual search comparisons will be much less than the total combinations, since the binary search – as implemented in the VLookup True and Match Option 1 methods – of a range of 114,652 rows in Ascending sequence can locate a match in a maximum of 17 comparisons (114,652 is near 2 to the 17th power).

A sequential row by row search, as implemented in the VLookup False and Match Option 0 methods will require about 10,420 X .5 X 114,652. Why? Because on the average there will be as many searches above the half way point in the range of 114,652 rows as there are below the half way point.

Search Speed Control Panel Application Buttons

The following segments briefly describe the code behind each of the ten buttons in the Search Speed Control Panel. Then, the code behind each button will be explained in full detail.

Button 1 – Sort 114,652 Records

When the user clicks the first button (Sort 114,652 Records), it takes around 3 seconds to perform the following functions that prepare worksheet

"MasterCustomerList" (the range to be searched), for all options of the VLookup, Match and Range.Find commands. Even though the Match Option 0 and VLookup False methods do not require the data to be in any special order, it is sorted so that the Match Option 1 and VLookup True methods will function properly.

1) Convert each value in the search argument column to the same format (i.e. if the search key is a Company ID and some Company ID's are only numeric and others are mixed text and numeric, format them all as Text.)

Note that if all the keys contain at least one Alpha character, this conversion is not necessary. Also, if all the keys are numeric (i.e. dollar values or measurements), then no conversion is necessary.

2) Sort the range to be searched in Ascending Sequence

3) Sequence check the range to make sure it adheres to Excel's special ascending sequence requirements

The procedure name used in the Visual Basic Editor attached to this button is SortTableToBeSearched().

Button 2 – Search Using Match Opt 1

The second button illustrates the lightning-fast Match Option 1 method. On my computer it executes in around 2 seconds. Option 1 of the Match method requires the range to be searched to be in ascending order using Excel's special sort sequence. Although it will either find an exact or the closest match less than the search argument, the surrounding code has been modified to only accept an exact match. Of all the methods available to search large ranges, this method is my recommendation. The code behind this button uses the Application.WorksheetFunction.Match method. The VBA Procedure name attached to this button is SearchUsingMatchOption1().

Button 3 – Match Opt 1

The third button also illustrates the lightning-fast Match Option 1 method. The VBA code and description of this method is almost identical to Button 2, except that the errors and "not found" conditions are handled in a different manner. The code behind this button uses the Application.Match method. The VBA Procedure name attached to this button is SearchUsingMatchOption1Alt().

Button 4 – Search Using Vlookup True

The fourth button illustrates the fastest option for the VLookup command, the True option. On my computer it executes in just over 2 seconds. The True option of the VLookup method requires the range to be searched to be in ascending order using Excel's special sort sequence. Although it will either find an exact or the closest match less than the search argument, the surrounding code has been modified to only accept an exact match. This method is not nearly as versatile as the Match Option 1 command, but if programmed properly, it can almost rival the speed of the Match command. The primary issue with the VLookup method is that it doesn't return a position or address of the item found, only a value. The code behind this button uses the Application.WorksheetFunction.VLookup method. The VBA Procedure name attached to this button is SearchUsingVlookupTrue().

Button 5 – Vlookup True

The fifth button also illustrates the Vlookup True option. The VBA code and description of this method is almost identical to Button 4, except that the errors and "not found" conditions are handled in a different manner. The code behind this button uses the Application.VLookup method. The VBA Procedure name attached to this button is SearchUsingVlookupTrueAlt().

Button 6 – Search Using Match Opt 0

The sixth button illustrates the Match Option 0 designed by Microsoft to only find exact matches. The primary advantage to this option is that the range being searched can be in any order, eliminating any sorting or sequence checking requirements. The method starts at the top of the range being searched and proceeds row by row until a match is found. It is much slower than the Match Option 1 if the range being searched is very large. If an exact match is not located, the method throws an error code indicating "not found:. The code behind this button uses the Application.WorksheetFunction.Match method. The

VBA Procedure name attached to this button is SearchUsingMatchOption0().

Button 7 – Match Opt 0

The seventh button also illustrates the Match Option 0. The VBA code and description of this method is almost identical to Button 6, except that the errors and "not found" conditions are handled in a different manner. The code behind this button uses the Application.Match method. The VBA Procedure name attached to this button is SearchUsingMatchOption0Alt().

Button 8 – Search Using VLookup False

The eighth button uses the False option of the VLookup command which will either find an Exact match or throw an unmatched error code. The primary advantage to this option is that the range being searched can be in any order, eliminating any sorting or sequence checking requirements. The method starts at the top of the range being searched and proceeds row by row until a match is found. However, the VLookup False is much slower than the Match Option 0, even though both methods search row by row. The code behind this button uses the Application.WorksheetFunction.VLookup method. The VBA Procedure name attached to this button is SearchUsingVlookupFalse().

Button 9 – Vlookup False

The ninth button also illustrates the VLookup False option. The VBA code and description of this method is almost identical to Button 8, except that the errors and "not found" conditions are handled in a different manner. The code behind this button uses the Application.VLookup method. The VBA Procedure name attached to this button is SearchUsingVlookupFalseAlt().

Button 10 – Search Using Range Find

The tenth and final button illustrates the Range.Find method. Any range object can be searched for matching items. This method is by far the slowest, and is almost impractical for large searches such as the one illustrated in the "Speed Search Control Panel and Timing Comparison" application. It starts at the first row of the range being searched and proceeds row by row until either a match is found or all rows have been searched.

The user can specify if an exact match is required (LookAt:=xlWhole) or a partial match is requested (LookAt:=xlPart).

The VBA Procedure name attached to this button is SearchUsingRangeFind().

PERFORMING STATISTICAL ANALYSIS USING FORMULAS

Weighted Averages

The weighted average is utilized in averaging values in cases where each of these values plays a smaller or larger role in the set. The table below shows a company's investment portfolio. For each portfolio fund, the whole value, as well as return on the investment, is also shown. Want we want to find is the total returns on this portfolio. Calculating the simple average will not be enough since each of these investments contributes different amounts to the total portfolio.

Calculating the weighted average, the % contribution of each investment concerning the portfolio's total value is multiplied by the rate of return of the investment. The SUMPRODUCT function does a great job of multiplying two different values and then adding up each of the results. The SUMPRODUCT function can take about 255 arguments, which are separated by commas; however, this formula only requires two arguments. =SUMPRODUCT ((C4:C8/$C$9) , D4:D8)

The 1st argument takes the value of each investment and then divides it by the whole value. This yields five percentages representing each investment's weight.

	A	B	C	D	E
1					
2					
3		Investment	Value	Return Rate	
4		Duffy Cap Fund	25,419.31	7.410%	
5		Roberto Bond Fund	72,021.35	2.500%	
6		Sparks Income fund	139,806.15	10.120%	
7		Ziff Investor Fund	97,440.65	4.400%	
8		Cowbsell International Fund	88,967.56	5.100%	
9		Weighted Average Return	423,655.02	6.292%	

When using the SUMPRODUCT function, each of the 1st argument's elements is multiplied by its corresponding element in the 2nd argument. C4/C9 is multiplied by D4, while that of C5/C9 is also multiplied by D4. When the five elements are multiplied, then the five products are summed up using the SUMPRODUCT function.

If we make use of AVERAGE to discover the average of these returns, then we will get 5.906%. This result is less than our weighted average because investments such as Sparks Income fund has an investment has higher return compared to the average as well as representing a bigger part of the portfolio.

Smoothening of Data Using Moving Averages

Moving averages are utilized in smoothening out data to present a better picture of the data's overall trend. This is very effective when data points lack a regular pattern. The figure below reveals some golf scores. People that know much about golf knows how scores can be so irregular for the different rounds.

We need to smoothen out the lows and highs to create a chart that reveals the progress of these scores. To achieve this, the scores' moving average can be calculated, and then these values plotted on the chart.

=IF(ROW()<12,NA(), AVERAGE(OFFSET(D4,-9,0,10,1)))

This formula utilizes some Excel functions to achieve this task. The IF function appears first, which gives the #N/A for the 1st 9 rows.

To return the mean of the initial ten scores, the AVERAGE function is used. About 255 arguments are taken by the AVERAGE function; however, only one needs to be supplied.

	A	B	C	D	E	F
			fx =IF(ROW()<12,NA(), AVERAGE(OFFSET(D4,-9,0,10,1)))			
1						
2						
3		Date	Course	Score	Moving Average	
4		5:13:2013	Tiburon Golf Club	98	#NA	
5		5:20:2013	Colbert Hills	88	#NA	
6		5:27:2013	Colbert Hills	84	#NA	
7		6:3:2013	Colbert Hills	94	#NA	
8		6:10:2013	Tiburon Golf Club	85	#NA	
9		6:17:2013	Tiburon Golf Club	88	#NA	

10	6:24:2013	Tiburon Golf Club	89	#NA	
11	7:1:2013	Iron Horse Golf Club	84	#NA	
12	7:8:2013	Tiburon Golf Club	84	#NA	
13	7:15:2013	Tiburon Golf Club	97	89.1	
14	7:22:2013	Tiburon Golf Club	97	89.0	
15	7:29:2013	Tiburon Golf Club	84	88.6	
16	8:5:2013	Iron Horse Golf Club	86	88.8	
17	8:12:2013	Tiburon Golf Club	89	88.3	
18	8:19:2013	Tiburon Golf Club	89	88.7	
19	8:26:2013	Tiburon Golf Club	93	89.2	
20	9:2:2013	Tiburon Golf Club	90	89.3	
21	9:9:2013	Tiburon	90	89.9	

		Golf Club			
22	9:16:2013	Tiburon Golf Club	85	90.0	
23	9:22:2013	Indian Creek Golf course	90	89.3	
24	9:30:2013	Iron Horse Golf Club	94	89.0	
25	10:7:2013	Indian Creek Golf course	93	89.9	
26	10:14:2013	Bent Tree	90	90.3	
27	10:21:2013	Indian Creek Golf course	100	91.4	
28					
29					
30					

The OFFSET function included is used in returning a given range, which offset from the beginning point. The OFFSET arguments are stated below:

Height: The number of rows that should be present in the returned range

Reference: That cell where this OFFSET function begins

Width: The number of columns that should be present in the returned range

Cols: These are the columns from the beginning cell. Positive numbers are counted to the right, while negative numbers are counted to the left.

Rows: These are the rows away from the beginning cell

If cell D13 is made the reference argument, the OFFSET begins its counting from here. The -9 present in the rows argument is telling OFFSET to begin its counting up by nine rows. The zero present in the cols argument means that the OFFSET function remains in that column.

The height argument is placed at 10, which means our range will have a height of 10 rows or D4:D13. 1, which is made the width argument maintains the range at just one column. The OFFSET function gives the result and what is converted into AVERAGE is the D4:D13 range

Creating Descriptive Statistics with the Use of Functions

Data can be presented in quantitative summaries when utilizing descriptive statistics. What you're producing when data is summed, counted, or averaged, is descriptive statistics. Here, we'll be considering some functions that can be used in profiling any set of data as well as ensure comparisons that can be utilized in some other analysis can be enabled.

Getting the smallest or largest value

The figure below tells the average high temperatures for each month for the Marietta city, Georgia. Here, we want to know those months having the lowest and highest average temperature. The formula below will tell the maximum average high temperature

=MAX (C4:C15)

					fx =MAX(C4:C15)		
	A	B	C	D	E	F
1						
2						
3		Month	Average High Temp			
4		JAN	31			
5		FEB	35		Max	Min
6		MAR	43		73	31
7		APR	50		Max Month	Min Month

8	MAY	59	JUL	JAN
9	JUN	65		
10	JUL	73		
11	AUG	69		
12	SEP	62		
13	OCT	51		
14	NOV	41		
15	DEC	34		
16				

The formula that comes after will bring back the month corresponding to the earlier formula's temperature. =INDEX(B4:B15,MATCH(E6,C4:C15,FALSE),1)

Two functions are provided by Excel to determine the smallest and largest values found in a range: MIN and MAX. The two formulas can accept about 255 arguments. The data we are working with is found in C4:C15, and this is the range passed into MIN and MAX. MAX returns the highest value in the range, which is 73, while MIN returns the smallest value, which is 31.

Calculation of Median, Mean and Mode

When referring to average, we are talking about the arithmetic mean. If we have some student's scores set at cell C4 to Cell 23. For mean, we use the AVERAGE function. To compute the median, mean, and mode for these scores, we use:

=MEDIAN (C4:C23)

=AVERAGE (C4:C23)

=MODE (C4:C23)

If there's a great difference between the MEDIAN and AVERAGE, it means the grades were not distributed evenly throughout the population. The MEDIAN returns the value that is in the center; if the number of grades is even in number, then we cannot get a particular value that claims the middle spot. So, in this case, we need to find the mean of the two values. The MODE gives you the grade that appears the most.

Data separation into percentiles

When data is separated into bins or buckets, we are providing insight into how each of these values is compared to the whole. The figure below reveals a list of workers processing a product and how much default per one thousand products. Here, we'll be trying to bucket the data to 4 bins to easily identify those performing well as well as those workers that may need additional training.

To compute this demarcation, Excel 19 has the QUARTILE function. A quartile is a type of bucket holding 25% of the whole data.

=QUARTILE ($C$4:$C$33,6-ROW(A2))

	A	B	C	D	E	F	G	H
				fx =QUARTILE ($C$4:$C$33,6-ROW(A2))				
1								
2								
3		Employee	Defects/1000	Quartile				
4		Adam John	47	1		Maximum	50.0	
5		Alex Cone	31	3		25th percentile	23.0	
6		Alfred Gonzalez	50	1		50th percentile	31.0	
7		Alyssa Clark	41	2		75th percentile	44.5	

8	Amelia Rose	30	3			
9	Anna Grace	30	3			
10	Audrey Love	23	4			
11	Chloe Brian	27	3			
12	Eli Brown	34	2			
13	Eric Green	48	1			
14	Evan Lucy	17	4			
15	Evelyn Salt	22	4			
16	Gabriel John	43	2			
17	Gabriella Daniel	45	1			
18	Genesis Stone	23	4			

19		Isabella Garcia	49	1			
20		Jaden Henry	50	1			
21		Jerry Palmer	19	4			
22		Joseph Arthur	17	4			
23		Katelyn Stark	31	3			
24		Kyle Walker	19	4			
25		Laura Allen	47	1			
26		Layla Lovren	47	1			
27		Lillian Marshall	27	3			
28		Mason Matthews	41	2			

29	Nathaniel Allen	42	2			
30	Samuel Gomez	21	4			
31	Sean Chavez	39	2			
32	Victoria Cox	20	4			
33	William Freeman	27	3			
34						

The QUARTILE function provides the demarcation lines. Cell D4's MATCH formula in the figure above will locate the quartile where the cell C3 value will fall into. This formula is now copied and used for the remaining values.

=MATCH (C4,$G$4:$G$7,-1)

This function picks some values as well as an integer that represents the quartile to return. Values accepted for the quart argument include Minimum value (0),

25th percentile (1), 50th percentile (2), 75th percentile (3), Maximum values (4).

If that quart argument does not fall into the 0-4 range, then it brings an error. Anytime the quart argument comes in decimal form, just the integer part of the decimal value is used.

Creation of Frequency Distribution

Quartiles are a well-known way of grouping data into buckets and bins; this is the major reason why Excel has a reliable QUARTILE function. In some cases, you may prefer grouping your data into your defined bins. Below is a list of invoices (just a part shown out of the 50) as well as the whole amount that was sold on every invoice. What we want to know is how common it will be for our customers to buy between $1 & $100 and so on.

The FREQUENCY function of Excel 19 will count the invoices falling within our defined bins.

=FREQUENCY (C4:C53,F4:F13)

The FREQUENCY function deals with two arguments: The data that needs to be categorized into bins as well as the numbers representing the bin's highest amount. First of all, the bin values should be entered in the F column. The formula is not affected by column E; it's simply here to show each bin's lower bound.

To input FREQUENCY into column G, first of all, highlight range G4:G13 then type in the formula. The FREQUENCY formula result reveals that most customers buy $200 - $300 for each visit.

SCENARIO BUILDING WITH ONE-WAY DATA TABLE

In business decisions, we often ask ourselves what-ifs: What if the interest rates increases by 2 percentage points? What if the purchase price can be negotiated down by $10,000? Moreover, we would like to compare different scenarios side-by-side. Excel provides such powerful capabilities with an convenient tool called Data Tables.

This functionality is part of a group under Analysis called "What-if". On a Mac, here is where you find it under Data:

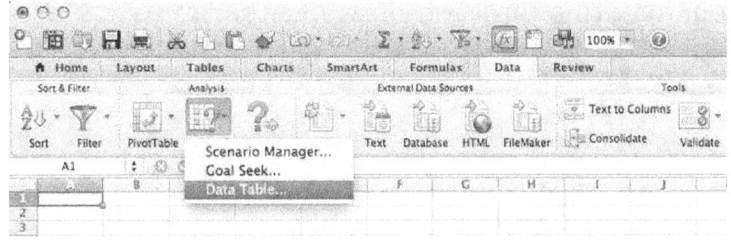

On a Windows PC, it is also under DATA:

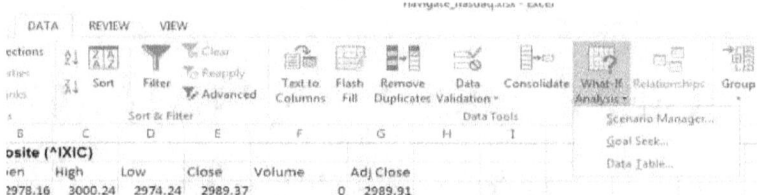

Now let us look at a simple example.

Example (Restaurant ratings: Scenario Analysis) A travel guide is updating its restaurant ratings in a town, which has 10 restaurants. It has collected numeric data, on a 0-100 scale on food quality, service quality, and dining environment of each of the dining places. Moreover, the weights for each of the dimensions are 40%, 30%, and 30%. Set up a spreadsheet to calculate their weighted scores.

Moreover, in order to get a comprehensive picture, set up a table to count how many of them are above 65, 70, 75, 80, 85, and 90, respectively.

Solution This problem has mentioned in an early module of this course. Below is the model.

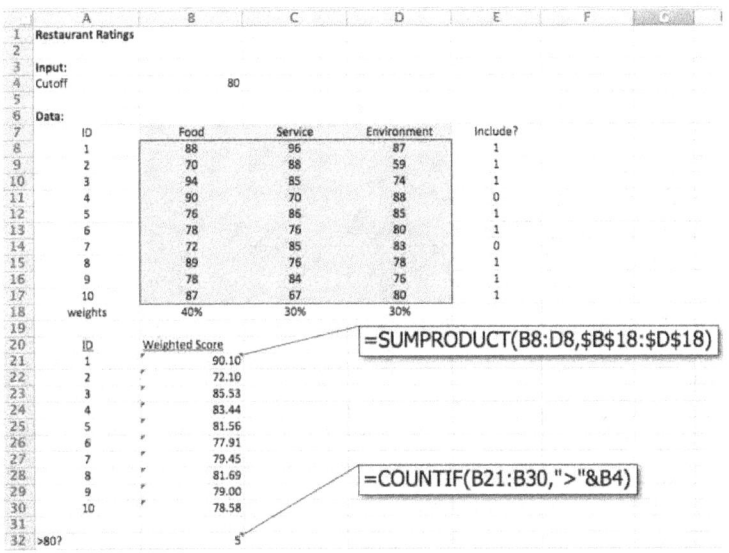

There we are only interested in how many scored above 80. Here, however, we need to do more. We could manually change the cutoff value (from 65 to 90, five times), and record the results for each cutoff. It will be great if we could automate the process and let Excel perform this scenario analysis on its own. Fortunately, Excel's Data Table does just that.

In here, we just need to vary one variable, i.e, the cutoff value, which is stored in a separate cell (B4). This allows us to do a one-way data table, whose procedures are as follows:

1- List all the cutoff values in one column;

2- In the header of the adjacent column over, define what output is here. Because we are interested in how many restaurant will cross a certain threshold, which is in cell B4, we just type =B32, as the following shows:

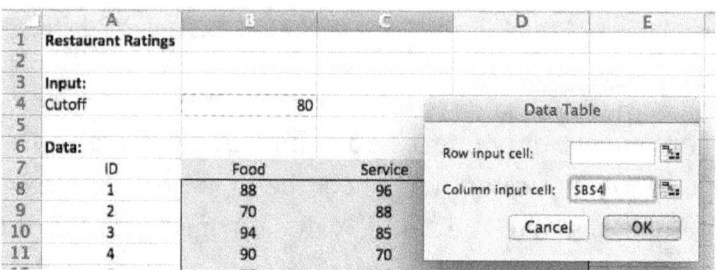

3- Select the entire table, including the header, and go to Data → What-if → Data Table, and the following window shows up.

This basically ask you where those scenarios of cutoff values should go into the model. The answer is cell B4, where the original cutoff value is stored. Because those scenarios are lined up in a column as we did in step 1, we leave "Row Input Cell" empty, and in "Column Input Cell" select cell B4. You will notice that Excel automatically adds $ signs to absolute reference that cell. After you click OK, the magic happens:

31				
32	>80?		5	
33				
34	Scenario Analysis			=B32
35			5	
36		70	10	
37		75	9	
38		80	5	
39		85	2	
40		90	1	
41				
42				

By now, you should be able to see what Data Table does. It is still the model's job to formulate a model and specify scenarios. But Excel can automate the calculation for each scenario, and produce the desired results for each scenario very quickly.

Then, let us look at an example, where it shows that you can output more than one variable of interests using one-way data table.

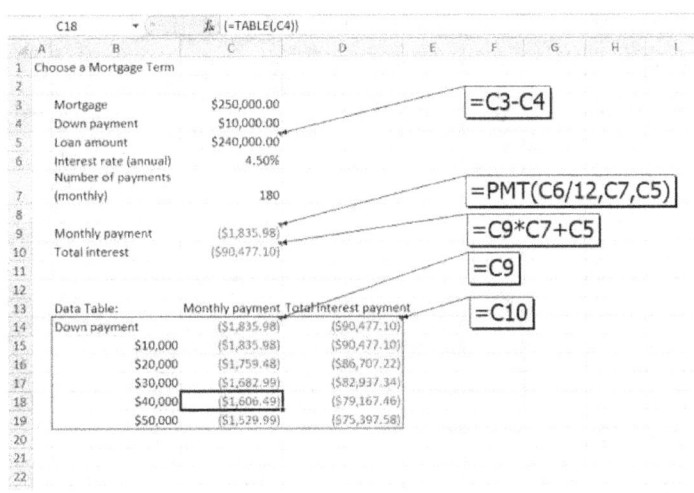

Solution Excel's Data Table is perfect for studying multiple scenarios in situations like this. Let us cover this step by step.

Step 1. We build up the proper model first. This is done in rows 3-9, which is an application of the PMT function, which we talked about earlier. As is shown there, if they pay down $10,000, their monthly payment is $1835.98, and the total interest payment is $90,477.10.

Step 2. Then, we set up the scenarios we are interested in studying. Here, they are about down payment, and there are five of them: $10,000, $20,000, $30,000, $40,000 or $50,000. We listed them in a column in B15-B19.

Step 3. The objectives are two: monthly payment and total interest. We use C14 and D14 to link back to our original model so that Excel knows what objectives the data tables are to compute. So in cell C14, we simply enter

=C9,

and in cell D14 we enter

=C10.

Step 4. Now we need to let Excel know what these scenarios are about and compute those monthly payment and interest payment for us. To do that, select the whole table in B14-D19 with your mouse, and then go to Data→ What-if Analysis, and then click on Data Table. The following dialog window will appear.

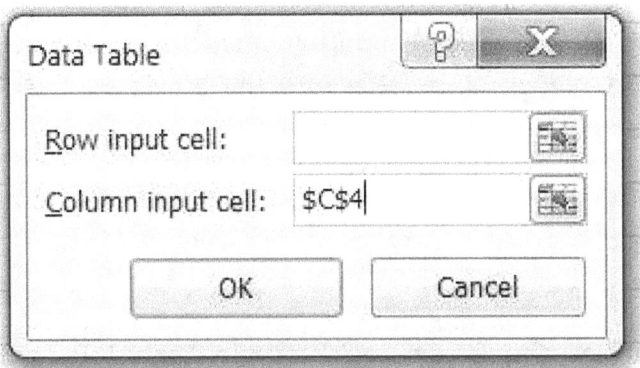

Here all our scenarios are in a column, and they all refer to different down payment in our original model. So enter $C$4 in the "Column input cell" field. Leave the "Row input cell" field empty. Once you click OK, new numbers will fill the table.

To check our results, as the down payment goes up, the monthly payment decreases. So does the total interest payment. This is indeed what we should expect. In fact, we can compute the difference for each increment in down payment: every $10,000 increase in down payment will decrease monthly payment by $76.50, and total interest payment by $3,769.88. With such analytics knowledge, now it is up to Mary and Joe to decide which down payment option to choose.

Note that, there are two different y-axis with different scales. This is because the magnitude of the series differ too much to be meaningfully presented in one figure (to see how to do add a second axis, check the visualize segment of this course). Nevertheless, the slopes of the two lines are exactly as we have anticipated: As one pays more down, her monthly payment as well as total interests goes down. Because the y-axis are negative numbers the chart shows a positive slope.

This following example shows that when the scenarios are built based on two different cells, separates data tables need to be built.

Example (Which Channel? Scenario Analysis) Tom, an aspiring author, has written a new novel and is using four channels to publish and distribute his writing. There are two large online channels (called A and B), an independent self-publishing channel (called C), and a physical store (called D). Each channel has its own fee structure, and each commands different market share (listed below).

	Online store A	Online Store B	Independent C	Physical Store D
Market share	73%	14%	12%	1%
Fee percentage	49%	30%	7.50%	35%

Suppose the novel will sell 1,000 copies, and Tom has decided to price it at $9.99. In addition to knowing the total revenue he gets from each channel, Tom is concerned with the following:

(1) He wants to know how his income would change if his top two channels (A and B) were to change their fee percentage.

(2) He is also curious as to how the overall demand will affect his revenue from all four channels.

Build a what-if analysis to answer Tom's questions.

Solution Before doing scenario analysis, we need to build a model. This model has been built and mentioned in the Build Models module of this course. So we will not repeat here, except to show the completed model here (from Row 1 to Row 12 in the picture below).

	A	B	C	D	E	F	G
1	Channel						
2							
3	Unit price	$9.99					
4	Total demand	1,000.00					
5							
6		Online store A	Online Store B	Independent C	Physical Store D		
7	Market share	73%	14%	12%	1%		
8	Fee percentage	49%	30%	7.50%	35%		
9							
10	Demand for each channel	730	140	120	10	=$B$4*E7	
11	Unit revenue from each channel	$5.09	$6.99	$9.24	$6.49	=$B$3*(1-E8)	
12	total revenue	$3,719.28	$979.02	$1,108.89	$64.94	=E10*E11	
13							
14							
15	Scenario Analysis: Fee Percentages						
16			Revenue A	=B12		Revenue B	=C12
17			$3,719.28			$979.02	
18		10%	$6,563.43		10%	$1,258.74	
19		15%	$6,198.80		15%	$1,188.81	
20		20%	$5,834.16		20%	$1,118.88	
21		25%	$5,469.53		25%	$1,048.95	
22		30%	$5,104.89		30%	$979.02	
23		35%	$4,740.26		35%	$909.09	
24		40%	$4,375.62		40%	$839.16	
25		45%	$4,010.99		45%	$769.23	
26		50%	$3,646.35		50%	$699.30	
27		55%	$3,281.72		55%	$629.37	
28		60%	$2,917.08		60%	$559.44	
29		65%	$2,552.45		65%	$489.51	
30		70%	$2,187.81		70%	$419.58	
31							

To answer the first question, we need to set up a one-way data table for fee percentages for channels A and

B. To do that, let us say they could vary between 10% to 70% for both channels, each in 5% increment, and list them out as two separate columns (in B18-B30, and D18-D30, respectively).

Then, we define our variables of interest. For channel A, it is the total revenue from A in cell B12. Therefore, in the top row of the data table (cell B17), we enter =B12.

The third step is to select the entire table (A17-B30), and go to Data→ What-if → Data table. Because those scenarios are about channel A's fee percentage in cell B12, we enter that as column input cell, and leave row input cell empty (see below).

You will see the table gets filled after your click on OK.

Repeat the same steps for channel B. Its column input cell should be C8, where the fee percentage of channel B is.

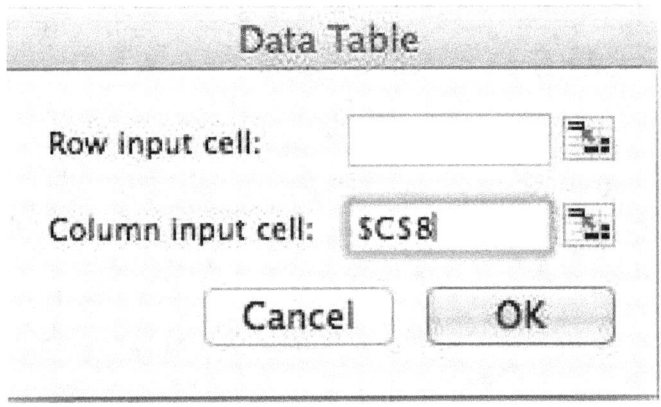

Now that we have the two tables, we can put them in one figure:

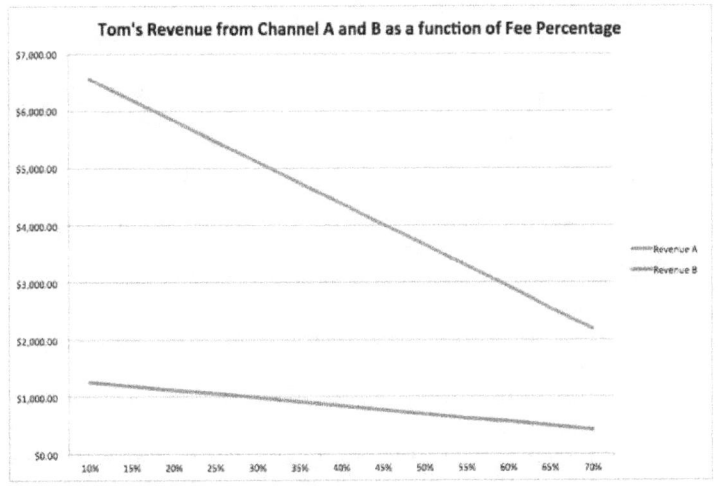

We can see that as the fee percentages for both channels go up, the authors get less revenue. Moreover, we see that the slope of decrease is steeper for channel A. In fact, from the data tables, we can compute the difference in revenue for each 5% increase in fees. For channel A, it is $364.63, and for channel B it is $69.93. Why?

The reason is apparent if we apply our modeling thinking and go back to our original model. The objective of total revenue from each channel is formulated as:

Revenue from a channel = Demand x unit revenue.

In our model, any fee change will not cause any change in demand, but it will affect unit revenue to the author which is formulated as:

Unit revenue = Unit price x (1 - fee percentage).

So, any 5% increase in fee will result in a reduction of unit revenue by $9.99 x 5% = $0.4995. Demand remains to be 1000 units x 73% market share = 730 units. Hence the net effect of change in total revenue from channel A is $0.4995 x 730 = $364.63.

Similarly for channel B, the net effect of change in total revenue is $0.4995 x (1000 x 14%) = $69.93.

The implication of this result is that the author's revenue is more sensitive to the channel that has the highest market share (i.e., channel A), therefore more attention needs to be paid on this key variable.

To answer the second question on the effect of overall demand, we follow the same procedure. To create scenarios, we vary demand from 300 up to 1800 with the increment of 100. This time, however, because all four quantities of interests (Revenue A, B, C, and D) are functions of the same demand, we only need one DataTable, as shown below.

	A	B	C	D	E	F	G
1	Which Channel?						
2							
3	Selling price	$9.99					
4	Total Demand	1000					
5							
6		Online store A	Online Store B	Independent C	Physical Store D		
7	Market share	73%	14%	12%	1%		
8	Fee percentage	49%	30%	7.50%	35%	=$B$4*E7	
9							
10	demand for each channel	730	140	120	10	=$B$3*(1-E8)	
11	unit revenue from each channel	$5.09	$6.99	$9.24	$6.49	=E10*E11	
12	total revenue	$3,719.28	$979.02	$1,108.89	$64.94		
13							
14		=B12	=C12	=D12	=E12		
15	Scenario analysis on demand:						
16	Demand	Revenue A	Revenue B	Revenue C	Revenue D		
17		$3,719.28	$979.02	$1,108.89	$64.94		
18	300	$1,115.78	$293.71	$332.67	$19.48		
19	400	$1,487.71	$391.61	$443.56	$25.97		
20	500	$1,859.64	$489.51	$554.45	$32.47		
21	600	$2,231.57	$587.41	$665.33	$38.96		
22	700	$2,603.49	$685.31	$776.22	$45.45		
23	800	$2,975.42	$783.22	$887.11	$51.95		
24	900	$3,347.35	$881.12	$998.00	$58.44		
25	1000	$3,719.28	$979.02	$1,108.89	$64.94		
26	1100	$4,091.20	$1,076.92	$1,219.78	$71.43		
27	1200	$4,463.13	$1,174.82	$1,330.67	$77.92		
28	1300	$4,835.06	$1,272.73	$1,441.56	$84.42		
29	1400	$5,206.99	$1,370.63	$1,552.45	$90.91		
30	1500	$5,578.92	$1,468.53	$1,663.34	$97.40		
31	1600	$5,950.84	$1,566.43	$1,774.22	$103.90		
32	1700	$6,322.77	$1,664.33	$1,885.11	$110.39		
33	1800	$6,694.70	$1,762.24	$1,996.00	$116.88		
34							

In row 17, we link the four variables to the original model. Then select the whole range of A17-E33, and go to Data Table, and select Demand (cell B4) as column input cell:

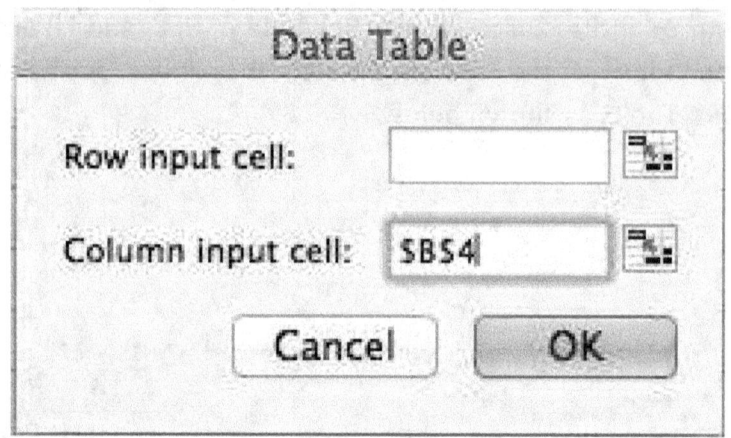

After the table is filled, we can then plot a line chart to visualize the effects (you can also use other techniques such as conditional formatting there we have covered in the Visualize module).

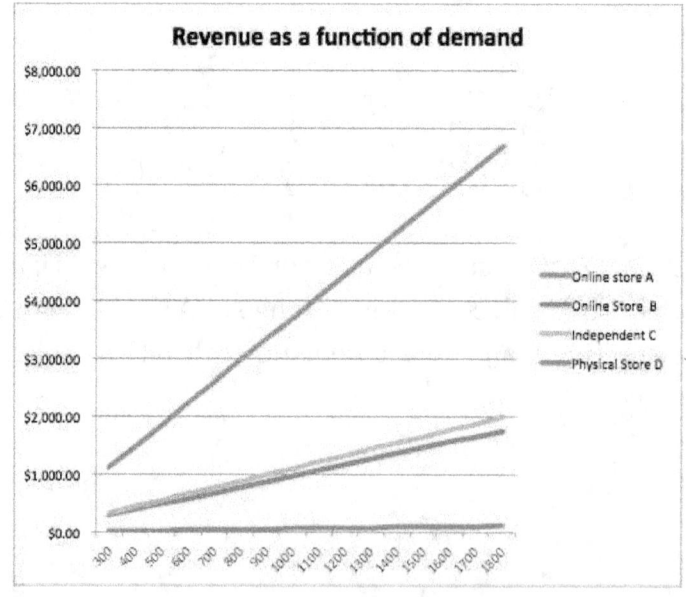

As expected, we see that because channel A has the largest market share, revenue from this channel is much more sensitive to demand changes. Since channel B and channel C have relatively small market share compared to channel A, their revenue impact is similar even though their fees differ quite a bit.

So far we have covered one-way Data Table: scenario studies on just one variable. Excel can also do two-way Data Table, considering simultaneous changes in two variables. Let's look at how it is done.

Exercise on one-way DataTable

1. In the channel example above, Tom is interested in seeing how his revenue may change with potential changes in channel A's market share (say, at 50%, 60%, 70%, 80% and 90%). Build a model to answer that.

2. In the restaurant rating example, repeat the one-way table analysis but this time calculate how many restaurants are (1) over each threshold and (2) have agreed to be included in the guide.

3. In the mortgage example, what is the impact of reducing number of payments on monthly mortgage payment and total interest amount?

AN EVENT MACRO

The VBA is an event-oriented language.

An event macro enables a macro to run automatically following certain events made in the manuscript, such as opening, closing, saving, double-clicking, changing and more.

A macro of this kind is written at the worksheet level or at the workbook level and not at the module level.

An event macro written at the worksheet level will apply only to the worksheet it was written in, while an event macro at the workbook level will apply to all the worksheets in the file.

Note:

The macro names are pre-determined and cannot be changed.

An event macro at the worksheet level

1. Double-click the name of the desired worksheet in the object explorer:
2. In the upper-left window select WorkSheet:
3. Choose the event that will run the code automatically from a list in the right window.

The following table lists the important events in the worksheet:

Macro:Action

Change:This macro will run automatically when a value in one of the worksheet cells changes

SelectionChange:This macro will run automatically when cells in the worksheet are selected

Note: when selecting an event macro of Change type, the reserved word Target will appear inside the brackets.

Target represents the range that triggered the event (contrary to ActiveCell that represents the active cell).

Run the following code to see the difference between Target and ActiveCell:

An event macro at the workbook level

1. Double-click ThisWorkBook:
2. In the left upper window, select Workbook:
3. Choose the event which will run the code automatically from the list in the right window.

The following table lists the important events in the workbook:

Open: This macro will run automatically when you open the workbook

BeforeClose: This macro will run before the file is closed (it enables the running of tests which prevent the file from being closed if pre-determined conditions were not fulfilled)

NewSheet: This macro will run when a new worksheet is added

BeforeSave: This macro will run before the file is saved

Deactivate: This macro will run when the workbook will become non-active (for example, when selecting a different file)

SheetChange: This macro will run when a change occurs in one of the worksheets

The above event macro is the Workbook_open type; in other words, this macro runs when the workbook is opened.

In this case, when the file opens, the second worksheet will open automatically.

Tip:

The following code cancels the workbook closure:

Supplements

How to protect the code from being viewed or copied

This protection blocks the unauthorized user from entering the code, looking at it or editing it.

1. Right-click on the project window (you can click anywhere in the project area).
2. Select VBAProject Properties.
3. In the open window, select the Protection tab:
4. Check 'Lock project for viewing'.
5. Enter password.
6. Any attempt to enter the VBA editor will open a window requesting a password:

Note:

The protection will only take effect after closing and reopening the file.

Recommendation:

It is recommended to use a password that you can easily remember when you will try to view the code in the future

Increase the macro running speed

Long codes that work on a large range of data slow the computer processing power.

One of the main reasons for that is that every action executed while the code is running actually takes place on the screen.

It is possible to make the code run without the screen refreshing:

At the beginning of the code write the command:

    Application.ScreenUpdating = False

Don't forget to return the screen to refresh at the end of the code by the command:

Application.ScreenUpdating = True

Calling a macro from another macro

You can run a macro from another macro. The call is made by writing the second code name inside the current one.

For example:

In the above example, running the code CallMacro, which calls the code MyMsg, will display a text box with the word "Hello".

Using the Microsoft Excel functions in a macro

Sometimes we want to use Excel functions in the macro we write. It is done by the Application.WorksheetFunction code, followed by the desired function name.

For example:

Range("a11").Value = _

Application.WorksheetFunction.Average(Range("a1:a10"))

Using colors

There are a few methods for choosing a color:

- By using the color name, for example vbRed.

- By using the index number of the color, for example ColorIndex=3:

    Range("a1").Interior.Color = vbRed

    Range("a2").Interior.ColorIndex = 26

    Range("a3").Font.Color = vbBlue

    Range("a4").Font.ColorIndex = 10

Basic list of colors

Index	Color
1	Black
2	White
3	Red
4	Green
5	Blue
6	Yellow

To find all the color codes (56 colors) you can write the following code, which colors the background of the cells in column A according to the index number of the color:

    For ColIndex = 1 To 56

    Cells(ColIndex, 1).Interior.ColorIndex = ColIndex

    Next

- By using the RGB code, for example:

ActiveCell.Interior.Color = RGB(200, 3, 8(

Remove modules

Right click on the module name and select Remove module.

If you choose to export it, the module will be saved in a ".bas" file.

Using the VBA Editor help

At any stage of the code writing, you can use help in two ways:

1. From the Help menu:
2. By writing a word in the VB editor and pressing F1.

Immediate window

This window enables you to run code lines for examination purposes, without needing to run them from the code itself.

This option is available only while there is no code running (if the code was not activated, or if it reached a breakpoint).

Displaying the variable value

To display the variable value, use the sign '?' (Question mark), and press Enter right after the command.

For example:

The above command will display the username as earlier defined in the software.

In the same way, the following command:

Will show the row number of the active cell.

Performing VBA commands

Type the command (without the question mark):

The above command will enter the value 10 into cell A1.

Note:

You can run only one command at a time.

Another option for getting information in a window is by using the command debug.print inside the code.

This command does not affect the running of the code itself, and its purpose is to send information to the Immediate window (make sure the window is displayed...).

Keyboard Shortcuts

Action Keys

    Displays the Help window   F1

    Displays the Object Browser   F2

    Displays the following search result, after closing the Search window   F3

Displays the last search result, after closing the Search window   Shift+F3

Displays the Properties window   F4

Runs the entire procedure   F5

Runs the procedure step-by-step   F8

Adds and removes a breakpoint in the line where the cursor is located   F9

Step Over - While running a code in a' step-by-step' mode, which calls to another code, this keyboard shortcut enables the external code to be run as a whole, without entering into it   Shift+F8

Runs the code to the point where the cursor is Ctrl+F8

Stops the code's running   Ctrl+Shift+F8

Removes all breakpoints   Ctrl+Shift+F9

Copy   Ctrl+C

Cut   Ctrl+X

Paste   Ctrl+V

Cut an entire row   Ctrl+Y

Displays the export code window   Ctrl+E

Displays the import code window   Ctrl+M

Displays the search window   Ctrl+F

Displays the immediate window   Ctrl+G

Displays the replace window   Ctrl+H

Displays the project explorer window   Ctrl+R

Cancels the last action   Ctrl+Z

Indents one line in   Tab

Indents one line out Shift+Tab

Go to the adjacent module   Ctrl+Tab

Stops the code from running (especially effective when the code enters an infinite loop and we want to stop its execution)   Ctrl+Break

Macros – Give Me the FAQs

"There is nothing more deceptive than an obvious fact."
– Sir Arthur Conan Doyle

The following are the most common questions I get about VBA

What is a Macro?

A Macro is a set of programming instructions that you can use to perform any task in Excel.

What is VBA?

VBA stands for Visual Basic for Applications. Visual Basic is a programming language Microsoft includes with each of their Office Products. It is the language you use to create Macros. The Basic language was originally created to allow anyone to write code. In fact the B in Basic stands for Beginner.

Why use it?

You can automate repetitive tasks or add new functionality to Excel.

Can you give an example?

Imagine you had to copy data from 10 different workbooks on a daily basis. Using VBA you could automate this using a simple procedure. Also it would run much quicker using VBA than you could do it manually.

What are the benefits?

You can save vast amounts of time on repetitive tasks. If you do the same task many times a week then you could create a Macro to do it for you.

It sounds good, are there any other benefits?

It can do complex tasks very quickly. For example comparing two worksheets with thousands of cells would take seconds with a Macro. It would take humans a lot longer.

You can also do things outside of Excel like send Emails, write to Databases, create XML files etc.

Tell me just one more benefit

VBA is compact. It has minimal impact on the workbook size and speed. Therefore if you replace complex formulas with VBA you can make your workbook smaller and faster.

Is it difficult to learn?

No. If you are learning VBA then you probably know Excel pretty well. VBA requires the same kind of mind set. All you need is to follow the steps and be willing to put in the time and effort. The good news is you can start as simple as you like and build as slow or fast as you like.

Where is the VBA Code stored?

Code is stored as part of the workbook file. It is stored as text. This is why it had minimal impact on the size of a workbook.

Which Version of Excel should I Use?

VBA is almost the same in versions of Excel 2007, 2010 and 2013. The examples in this writing should work with all these versions

THE MACRO RECORDER

One of the most important tools you can use as an Excel developer is the Macro Recorder. The macro recorder acts like a built-in programmer, and generates VBA code in a module inside the VBE that mimics what you do when recording the macro from the main Excel interface. The code generated by the macro recorder is by no means optimal. It can be clumsy and repetitive and doesn't use many of the powerful looping statements available in VBA.

That being said, it's a great way to find out which properties and objects are used to accomplish your goals. After looking back at the code generated, most professional developers significantly modify the code or just incorporate portions of the recorded statements into an existing application.

Launching The Macro Recorder In Excel 2003

Let's start with a simple example of recording a macro that will copy cells A1 through E10 from Sheet1 to cell F1 in Sheet2. These are the steps:

1) First, place some data in cells A1 through E10 of Sheet1.

2) To make sure that the macro will run, we need to set the security settings. From the menu bar, select Tools, Macro, Security

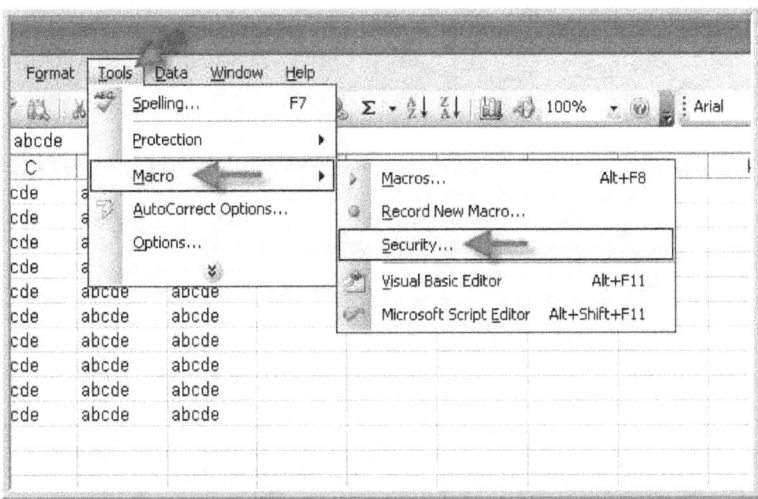

3) Set the security level to low.

4) From the menu bar, start recording the macro by selecting Tools, Macro, Record New Macro.

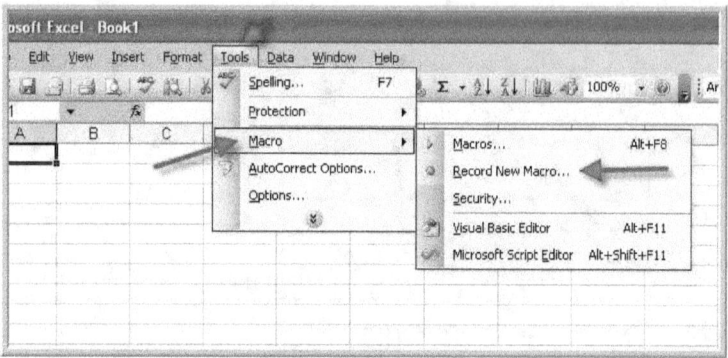

5) We will not be discussing those options at this point.

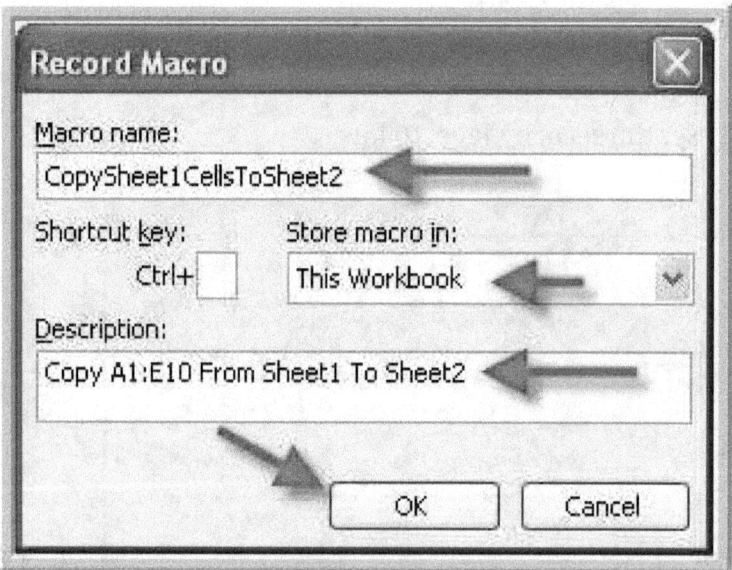

6) If you don't see the "Stop Recording" icon listed below, then you can enable it. It is not necessary, however, to use the "Stop Recording" icon because you can stop recording from the regular menu bar options.

7) In case you DO want to enable the "Stop Recording" icon, then go to the menu bar, select View, Toolbars, and then put a checkmark beside "Stop Recording".

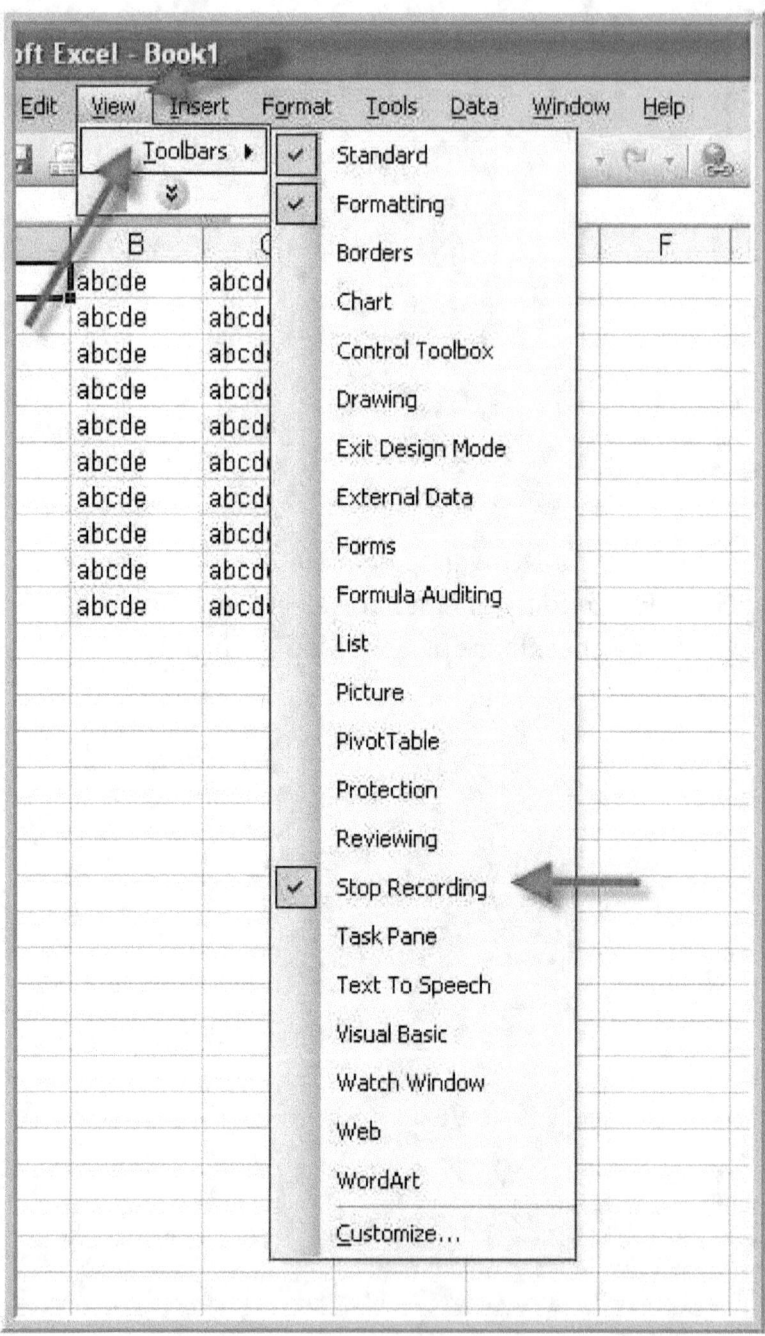

8) You are now ready to record your actions. In Sheet1, click on cell A1 and drag it down to cell E10. The entire rectangular area will be selected.

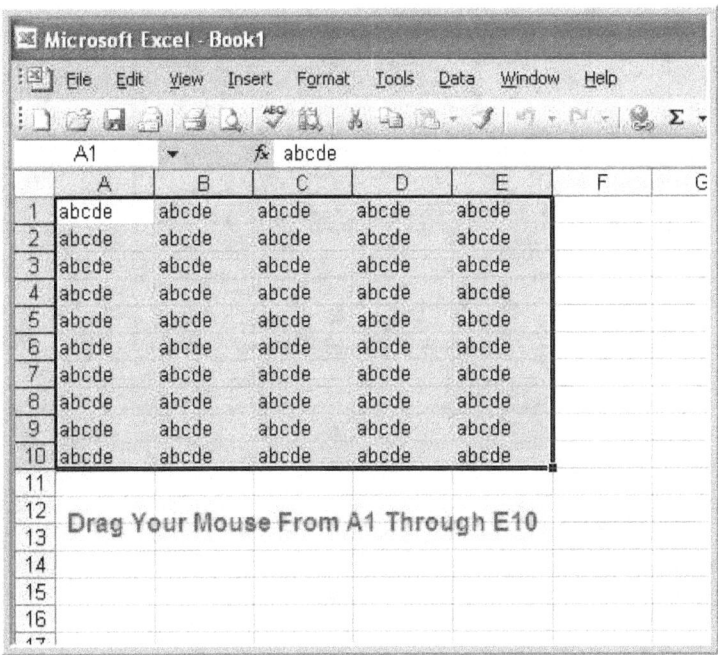

9) Either do a Ctrl-C (Control Key + the letter C) or from the menu bar, select Edit, Copy.

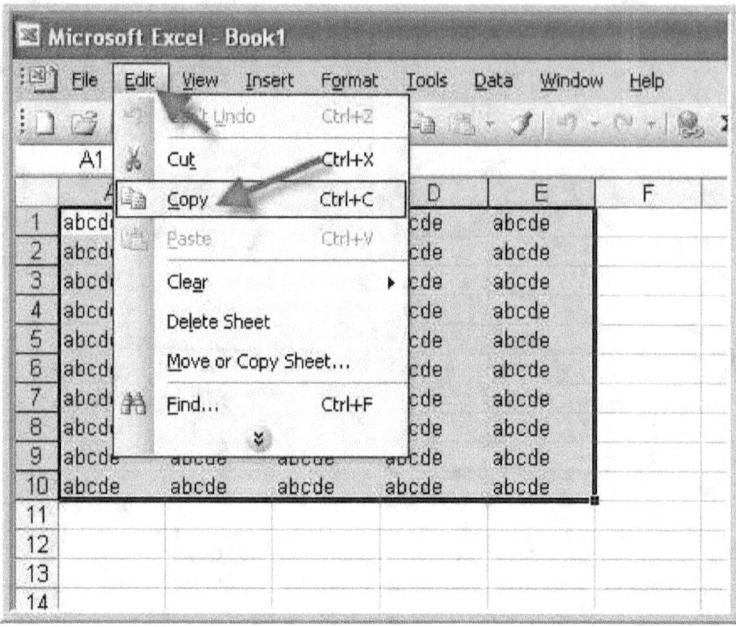

10) Switch to Sheet2. Select Cell F1. Then from the menu bar, select Edit, Paste. Your data will be pasted into Sheet2 starting with cell F1.

11) Now, in Sheet2, click on cell A1.

12) Switch to Sheet1. Notice that the selected cells still have the active copy status. Press the ESC key and click on cell A1 in Sheet1.

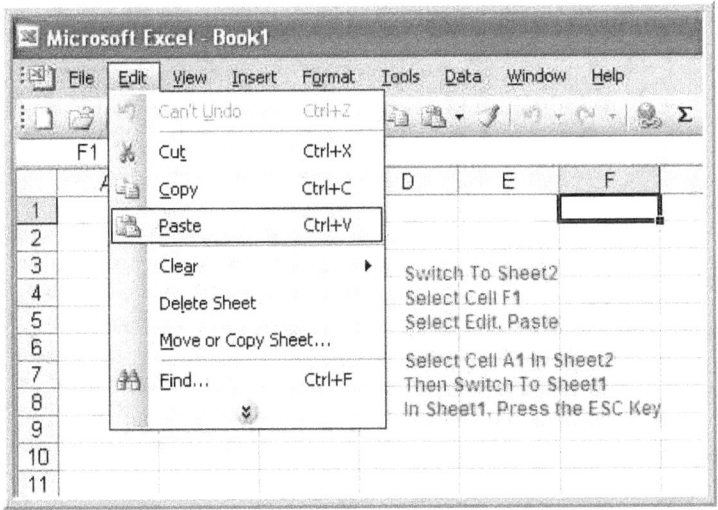

13) You have performed all the actions you required, so now you are ready to stop recording the macro. Either use the "Stop Recording" icon, or from the menu bar, select Tools, Macro, Stop Recording. As soon as you do this, your macro will appear in the VBE within a module.

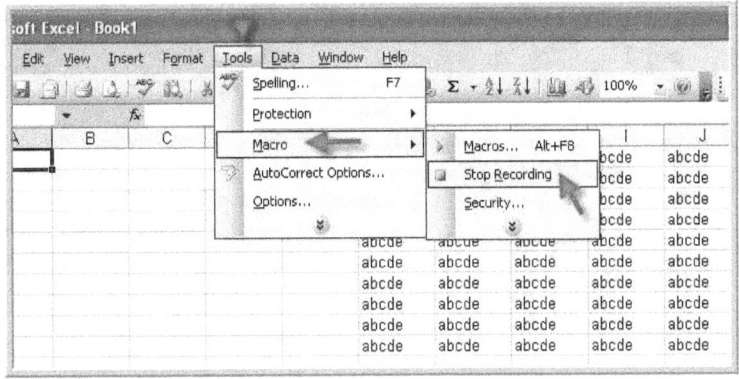

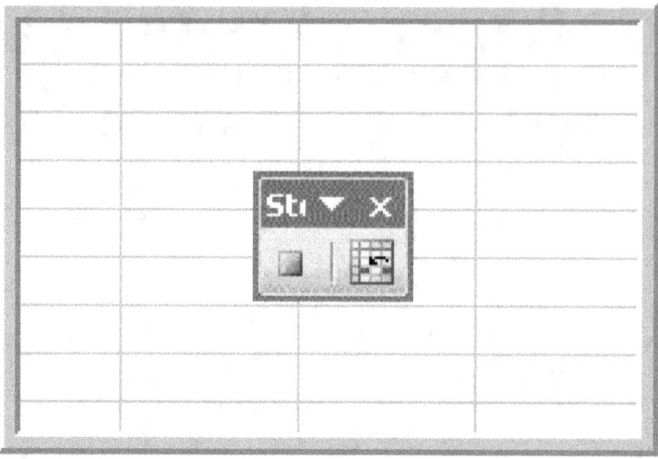

14) The code generated appears as follows:

```
(General)
Sub CopySheet1CellsToSheet2()
'
' CopySheet1CellsToSheet2 Macro
' Copy A1:E10 From Sheet1 To Sheet2
'

    Range("A1:E10").Select
    Selection.Copy
    Sheets("Sheet2").Select
    Range("F1").Select
    ActiveSheet.Paste
    Range("A1").Select
    Sheets("Sheet1").Select
    Range("A1").Select
    Application.CutCopyMode = False
End Sub
```

15) A professional developer would replace all the code above with a much simpler version:

```
Sub CopySheet1CellsToSheet2Simple()
```

ThisWorkbook.Sheets("Sheet1").Range("A1:E10").Copy ThisWorkbook.Sheets("Sheet2").Range("F1")

End Sub

The single statement used to copy cells A1:E10 from Sheet1 to Sheet2 explicitly references the workbook and worksheet names of the cells that are copied. Another method, using workbook and worksheet variables, will be described shortly in detail but the following example gives you a view. While using workbook and worksheet variables increases the number of statements, it is the best way to code for more complex applications. Here's the same copy function, but coded with workbook and worksheet variables:

```
Sub CopySheet1CellsToSheet2WithVar()

    Dim wkbCopyExample As Workbook

    Dim wksSourceWorksheet As Worksheet

    Dim wksTargetWorksheet As Worksheet

    Set wkbCopyExample = ThisWorkbook

    Set wksSourceWorksheet = wkbCopyExample.Sheets("Sheet1")

    Set wksTargetWorksheet = wkbCopyExample.Sheets("Sheet2")
```

```
wksSourceWorksheet.Range("A1:E10").Copy
wksTargetWorksheet.Range("F1")
```

End Sub

Launching The Macro Recorder In Excel 2007, 2010 and 2013

We will use the same example as we did for Excel 2003 - recording a macro that will copy cells A1 through E10 from Sheet1 to cell F1 in Sheet2. These are the steps from your Excel 2007/2010/2013:

1) Open a new blank workbook

2) Place some data in cells A1 through E10 of Sheet1

3) Save the workbook as a macro-enabled workbook using any name you choose by selecting the File tab, then Save As, and change the file type to macro-enabled workbook:

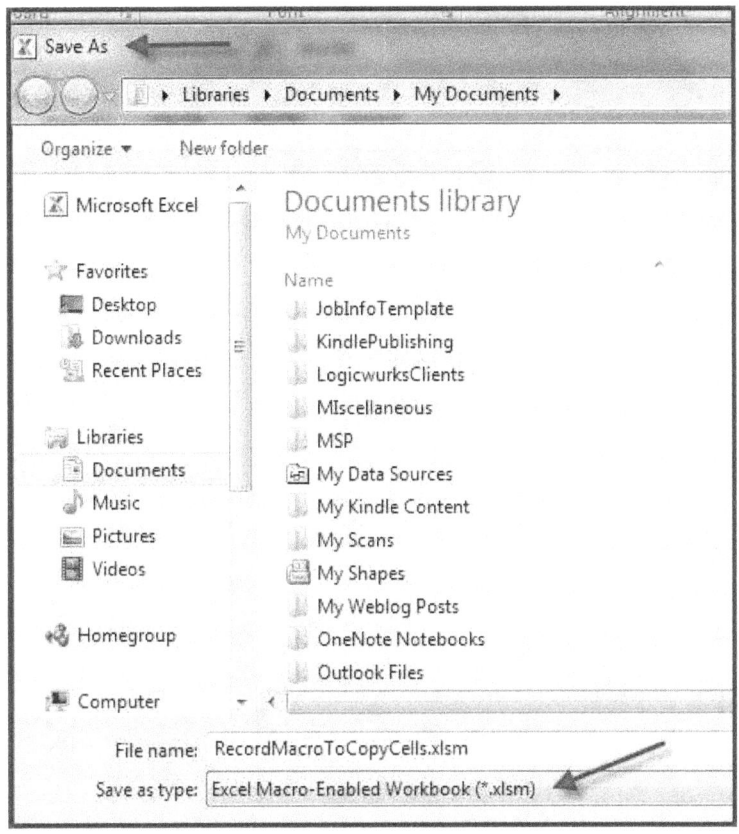

4) Start recording the macro by using the "Start Macro Recording" button in the lower left portion of your screen. (You can also use the "Record Macro" button in the Ribbon's Developer Tab or the "Record Macro" button in the Ribbon's View Tab...it's hiding underneath the "Macros" button as a drop-down).

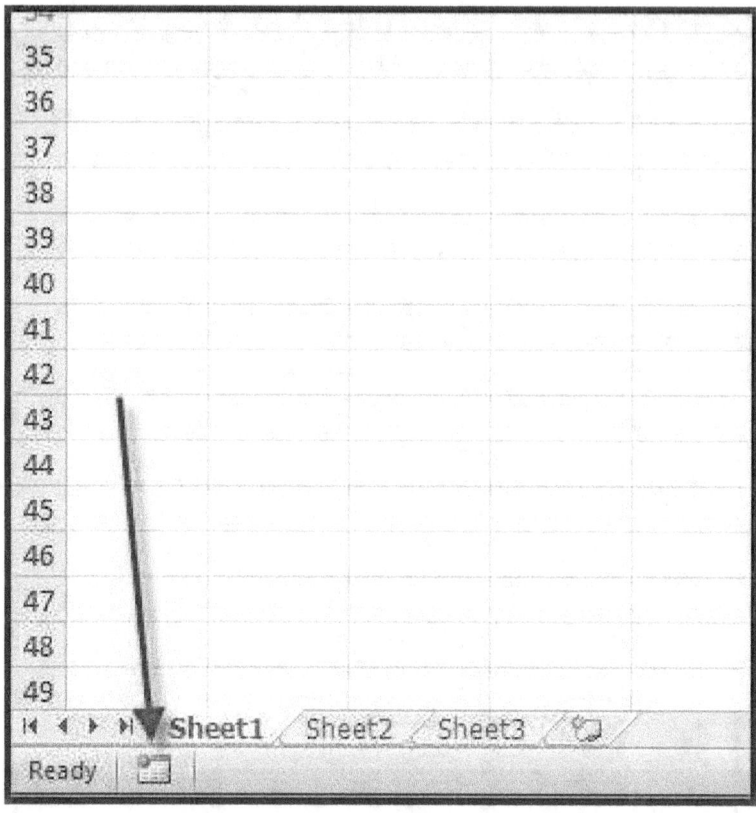

5) We will not be discussing those options at this point.

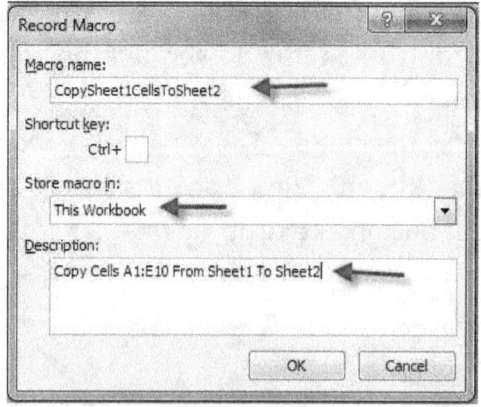

6) You are now ready to record your actions. In Sheet1, click on cell A1 and drag it down to cell E10. The entire rectangular area will be selected.

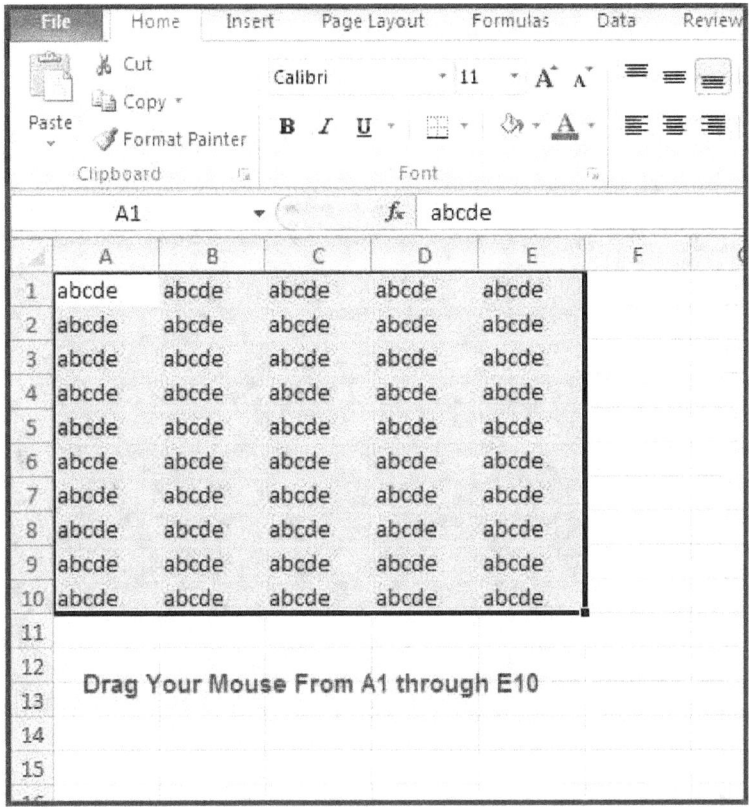

7) Either do a Ctrl-C (Control Key + the letter C) or use the Copy button in the Ribbon's Home Tab.

8) Switch to Sheet2. Select Cell F1. Then either do a Ctrl-V or use the Paste button in the Ribbon's Home Tab. Your data will be pasted into Sheet2 starting with cell F1.

9) Now, in Sheet2, click on cell A1.

10) Switch to Sheet1. Notice that the selected cells still have the active copy status. Press the ESC key and then click on cell A1 in Sheet1.

11) You have performed all the actions you required, so now you are ready to stop recording the macro. Use the "Stop Recording" button in the lower left of your screen to stop the recording.

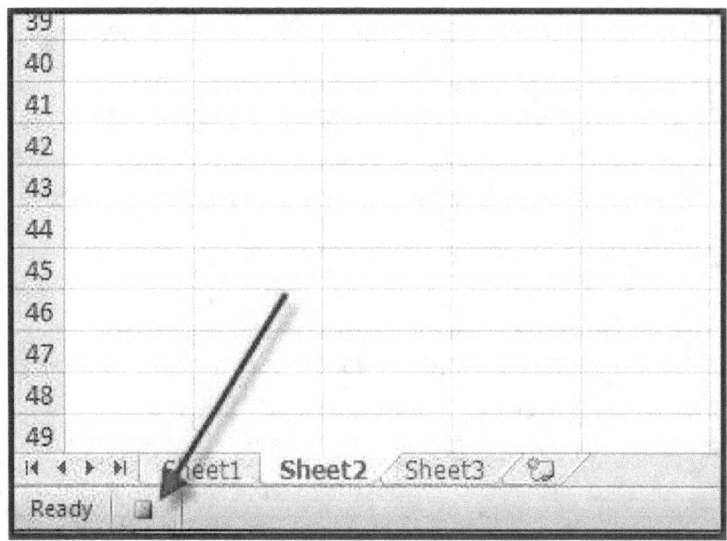

12) As soon as you do this, your macro will appear in the VBE within a module. The code generated appears as follows:

```
(General)
    Sub CopySheet1CellsToSheet2()
    
    ' CopySheet1CellsToSheet2 Macro
    ' Copy A1:E10 From Sheet1 To Sheet2
    
    
        Range("A1:E10").Select
        Selection.Copy
        Sheets("Sheet2").Select
        Range("F1").Select
        ActiveSheet.Paste
        Range("A1").Select
        Sheets("Sheet1").Select
        Range("A1").Select
        Application.CutCopyMode = False
    End Sub
```

13) A professional developer would replace all the code above with a much simpler version:

    Sub CopySheet1CellsToSheet2Simple()

        ThisWorkbook.Sheets("Sheet1").Range(" A1:E10").Copy
        ThisWorkbook.Sheets("Sheet2").Range(" F1")

    End Sub

The single statement used to copy cells A1:E10 from Sheet1 to Sheet2 explicitly references the workbook and worksheet names of the cells that are copied. Another method, using workbook and worksheet variables, will be described shortly in detail but the following example gives you a view. While using workbook and worksheet variables increases the number of statements, it is the best way to code for more complex applications. Here's the same copy function, but coded with workbook and worksheet variables:

```
Sub CopySheet1CellsToSheet2WithVar()

    Dim wkbCopyExample As Workbook

    Dim wksSourceWorksheet As Worksheet

    Dim wksTargetWorksheet As Worksheet

    Set wkbCopyExample = ThisWorkbook

    Set wksSourceWorksheet = wkbCopyExample.Sheets("Sheet1")

    Set wksTargetWorksheet = wkbCopyExample.Sheets("Sheet2")

    wksSourceWorksheet.Range("A1:E10").Copy wksTargetWorksheet.Range("F1")

End Sub
```

THE EXCEL OBJECT MODEL

As you use Excel, you probably see the workbooks, worksheets, and ranges as part of the application and not as individual objects. Internally, however, Excel treats these parts as individual, self-contained, objects in a hierarchical model called the Excel Object Model. You can take advantage of these objects to create VBA solutions without having to write too much code.

Objects and Collections

In programming or software, objects are packaged functionality with a defined set of behaviours (known as methods in VBA) and characteristics (known as properties in VBA). You can put various objects together to create solutions programmatically.

A collection is an object that groups several related objects together so that they can be programmatically controlled as a unit. A collection can have zero or more related objects. For example, there is a Worksheets collection which can hold several Worksheet objects. Each Worksheet object in the collection has its own properties and methods. However, the Worksheets collection also has its own properties and methods that you can use to control multiple Worksheet objects within it as a single unit.

The Object Hierarchy

The Excel object model is a structured model with different objects organised into a hierarchy based on the relationships between the objects. The object model defines which objects are exposed and how they relate to each other. The highest object in the hierarchy is Application, which represents the Excel application itself.

The image below shows a subset of the Excel object model. A rectangle represents a collection of objects and an oval represents a single object.

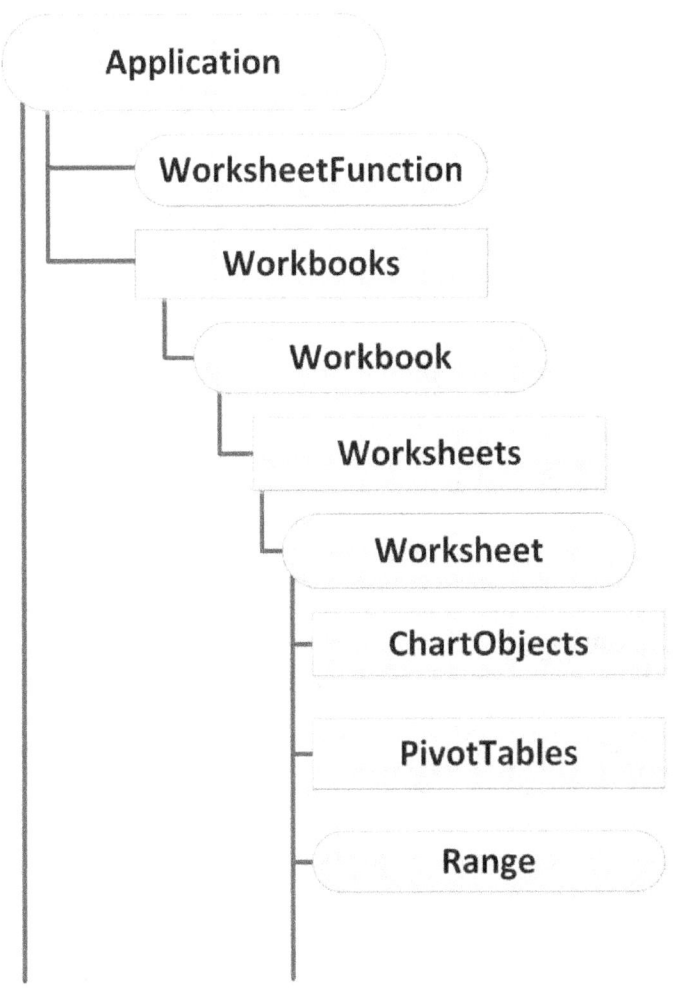

You can use the pre-packaged functionality in Excel objects to create custom solutions without having to write the code from scratch. For example, you may want to create a solution that uses the PivotTable object in Excel to display data to the user. You don't have to write the code to create a pivot table from scratch. That would be way too daunting! Instead, you can declare a

PivotTable object and access the functionality that's already built into it.

Declaring an Object

To create an instance of an object to access its methods and properties, you must first declare it as an object variable in your procedure.

For example, the following code declares rngVAT as a Range object variable:

Dim rngVAT As Range

If you intend to use an object in multiple places in your code, you can assign it to an object variable using the Set command. This makes for a cleaner and more efficient code. The following example assigns a range named Vat to a variable using Set:

Set rngVAT = Workbooks("AnnualFigures.xlsx")

Worksheets("Sheet1").Range("Vat")

We can then access properties and methods of the object using the variable, like in the example below:

rngVAT.Value = 0.2

You can also declare an object variable and use it in a For...Each loop to iterate through a collection to access instances of the object. In the example below, we loop through a collection (which is a range of selected cells) and use a Debug.Print statement to display the value of each cell in the Immediate window.

```
Dim rngCell As Range

For Each rngCell In Selection.Cells

    Debug.Print rngCell.Value

Next rngCell
```

```
Sub cellsText()

    Dim rngCell As Range

    For Each rngCell In Selection.Cells

        Debug.Print rngCell.Value

    Next rngCell

End Sub
```

Immediate

```
Theresa Sanchez
Alice Morgan
Steven Ross
Craig Griffin
Johnny Henderson
Jose Baker
Maria Anderson
Henry White
Anne Washington
Wanda James
```

Properties and Methods

To access the functionality provided by objects, you work with properties and methods.

Properties

Properties are a set of characteristics of an object. For example, the Worksheet object has properties like Name and Visible.

Methods

Methods are behaviours that an object can exhibit. These are actions that you can carry out with an object. For example, the Worksheet object has methods like ShowAllData, Protect and Calculate.

Tip: To get a detailed list of the methods and properties of an Excel object. Use the format "object name properties" or "object name methods" to search for it in your search engine, where object name is the name of the object for which you want help. One of the top search results will be the official VBA help page for that object.

Setting Properties and Calling Methods

To change the characteristics or attributes of an object, you change its properties by assigning different values to them. Methods, on the other hand, cause an object to carry out an action or a task. Hence, you use methods to perform actions and use properties to set or retrieve attributes of an object.

Setting Properties

To set a property of an object in code, use the following syntax:

Object.Property = Value

The following example assigns True to the Bold property of the Font object of the selected range. This bolds the text in that range.

Selection.Font.Bold = True

To turn off bold you can set the property to False, like this.

Selection.Font.Bold = True

Calling Methods

The way you invoke methods in your code will depend on whether the method returns a value and if that value will be used in your procedure. You can think of methods as verbs. For example, you can open a door. So, if we were to translate that to VBA code, it would be:

Door.Open

Some methods return a value and others don't. Also, some methods have parameters and others don't.

Note: A parameter is a variable that is part of a method's definition or syntax. When you call the method in your code, the values you pass into the parameters are called arguments. These terms are sometimes used interchangeably.

If you don't want to use the value returned by a method, or if the method doesn't return a value, then use the syntax below to call it. Note that the arguments are optional as not all methods have parameters.

Object.Method [arg1, arg2, ...]

An example of a method that does not have a parameter or a return value is the Select method of the Range object:

Range("A1:A10").Select

The following statement runs the AutoFit method of the Columns collection to auto-fit the text in the selected columns.

Selection.Columns.AutoFit

If a method returns a value, then you call it by assigning the return value to a variable.

If the method has parameters, then you place parentheses around the arguments when you call it. You generally want to use parentheses any time the method appears to the right of the equal sign.

Use the following syntax to call a method when you want to assign the return value to a variable:

Variable = Object.Method([arg1, arg2, ...])

You can also explicitly define a parameter by assigning an argument directly to its name when you call the method. The following example copies data from cells A1:A4 on Sheet1 to cells B1:B4 on Sheet1. You can see that the Destination parameter was explicitly defined.

```
Sub CopyAndPaste()

    Worksheets("Sheet1").Range("A1:A4").Copy

    ActiveSheet.Paste Destination:=Worksheets("Sheet1").Range("B1:B4")

End Sub
```

Using the With...End With Statement

The With...End With statement is something you will encounter often when you're editing macros generated by the macro recorder. This statement is used primarily to access properties and methods of objects.

When you access properties and call methods, you will often write several statements that perform actions on the same object. You can use the With...End With statement to make the code run more efficiently as you're referencing the object name just once.

The following piece of code sets various formatting options for the selected range in Excel using the With...End With statement.

```
Sub UsingWith()

' Formats the selected range in the active worksheet.

    With

        Selection.Font

            .Name = "Calibri"
```

```
        .Size = 20
        .Bold = True
        .Italic = True
        .Underline = True
    End With
End Sub
```

DERIVED DATA TYPES IN VBA

Here, we introduce derived data types in VBA, namely enumeration, and custom. The custom data types represent a vital data structure which permits one to deal with complex systems that reduce and simplify the code. Enumerated data types are not as complicated as custom data types. Instead, they have a simple data structure which creates codes that are readable.

VBA Custom Data Types

Having a single name, these data types are a collection of related elements of different types. An example is an application that stores and displays customer information found in a database. The database has related information such as age, address, identification number, and name. You may declare five different variables for each of these particular variables, but that would eventually prove to be cumbersome. In fact, the program would end up being longer and less efficient, not to mention difficult to read and difficult to write. Type and End type statements are used to define custom data types. You can see these below:

```
Public Type CustomerInfo
ID As Integer
Name As String * 30
Age As Integer
Gender As String * 1
Address As String * 50
End Type
```

In the example shown above, we have the name CustomerInfo given to a custom data type containing five elements. It is important to make sure that a custom data type definition is done in the general declaration module.

It is also essential that one differentiates between custom data type definition and variable declaration. The variable declaration describes the type of data but not the variable. This means that data is not shown by the custom data type. Therefore, it is okay to assign a public scope to the custom data type.

In the same way, you may want to declare an integer variable to your program's entirety, you may similarly wish to have variables of custom data type in the whole program.

Declaring a variable of type CustomerInfo is not different from a regular variable declaration. In the example below, the declaration results in the creation of a CustomerInfo variable called "customer."

```
Dim customer As CustomerInfo
```

To access individual elements of the custom data type, we use the dot (.) operator. This has been illustrated below:

```
customer.ID = 1234
customer.Name = "Fred Flintstone"
customer.Gender = "M"
customer.Age = 40
```

Other things that one can perform with custom data type include defining elements as arrays, declaring variable arrays, and passing elements of variables to procedures.

Enumerated Types

Enumerated types have several elements, and this data type originates from an integer data type. In this data type, every integer is assigned an identifier. The names of the enumerated types are constants. A constant will allow one to use symbols instead of numbers. This improves the readability of the program.

To define enumerated data types, it is a must to have its elements arranged between Enum and End Enum statements. Below is an example to demonstrate the definition of enumerated data types:

```
Public Enum Weekdays
Sunday = 1
Monday
Tuesday
Wednesday
Thursday
Friday
Saturday
End Enum
```

Within the Enum statement, all elements of an enumerated data type are assigned a constant value. The elements can have both positive and negative integers. When there is no exact initialization done, VBA automatically gives the first element the value 0, the other element the value 1, and so forth.

To declare the variables of an enumerated type, we have to use its name. We can assign them any integer value; however, there will be no point of having an enumerated type if we allocate the variable enumerate constant.

BEYOND THE BASICS

Microsoft's Excel VBA is a very much like an iceberg. No matter how basic the function is, you will inevitably come across a more complex form of it shortly. So, when it comes to creating your own macros, there is much more involved than what can readily meet the eye.

When building a macro, there are quite a few things you must keep in mind. By following some of these basic rules, you can truly simplify your venture into the macro world but at the same time, leave yourself open to learn new things.

Rule #1: Keep it simple

It is one thing to write code in practice where you are free to make mistakes and find the time to fix them. But when you are learning something new, it is extremely important that you do a trial run of any macro you make before you decide to launch it live. To that end make sure that your practice macro is simple. So if you need to write code that will allow you to automate the updates of a hundred worksheets your practice macro should be to update one. If you need a macro to automate a hundred cells, then limit your practice macro to update five.

By approaching your code in this way, it will be easier for you to catch errors and modify it whenever needed. Once you have mastered the code and it is working as you expect, you can always expand it to match your immediate needs. Here is a sample of the order of getting a macro live.

1. Create your new workbook
2. Add some sample data
3. Build your new macro
4. Do a test run
5. Fix any errors
6. Create a copy
7. Add your code to your active workbook
8. Retest the macro with the new data
9. Fix any errors
10. Create a backup copy
11. Test your macro
12. Fix any errors
13. Go live

This may seem like a lot of repetitive busy work, but these rules are very practical. Errors are a very real part of a programmers life, and you should expect to have more than your share of them. It is much better though, to have an error in a practice session than in a live code that could compromise the data you have.

These steps are relatively easy to do and the more successful you are at it, the more confidence you will have when you are creating macros in real life. Never be afraid of making a mistake. Even if you can't find the error having a backup copy makes it possible for you to always go back to a safe place and start again without risk of losing data.

Keep reading: There is a lot to know about using Excel VBA, and you will likely remember those codes, syntaxes, functions, loops variables, arrays, etc. that you use frequently, however, by making sure that you keep abreast of what can be done with VBA you will be able to stay ahead of the game.

Keep a glossary of terms around until you can remember them all by heart. There are many that you will have to rely on as you continue to grow in your learning of VBA.

Rule #2: Always leave comments in your code. This will serve as a reminder so that when you look at it (perhaps in a few months), you know what your intended purpose was.

Rule#3: Name your variables in a way that they will mean something to you. This practice serves not just as a memory device, but it's also protection. It will keep you from mistakenly applying the wrong code to a particular variable.

Rule #4: Whenever you see a code like "MyWorkbooks.Worksheets("Sheet1"), remember that it can be substituted with the actual name of the worksheet itself.

Rule #5: Whenever you are working with large amounts of data first, copy the values of the cells to an array. Then you will be able to manipulate them, which will be a much faster process than trying to address each cell one at a time.

Rule #6: When you write a new macro always create a copy of the workbook first. This way, you reduce the risk of accidentally deleting the data.

Rule #7: For new macros, make sure you divide the task up into smaller bite-sized pieces. Then, tackle each of them one at a time. Get the first one working smoothly and then move onto another one. Test each phase of the code for errors before you begin working on another piece of the puzzle.

Rule #8: Before starting a new project, turn on the OPTION EXPLICIT button at the top of the module. When on, you are required to declare a variable before you start work. To do this go to your menu bar and select "Tool", the "Options", and then check the box for "Require Variable Declaration".

Rule #9: When creating a new macro start by setting up a few sample products before you apply your new code with actual data. You can learn many different details about writing code in VBA, but just like learning a new language, the only way you can cement them in your mind is to create and run macros in much the same way you would practice reading, writing, and speaking in your new tongue. Whether you choose to create your sample data for yourself or you want to test your new code with smaller projects, it is a necessary part of life with VBA to test the waters first. By doing this, your skills in VBA will improve much faster than if you just try to master it by studying alone.

These are just a few basic guidelines you need to keep in mind when learning VBA. While some of these rules seem pretty obvious, it is easy to forget them when you are overwhelmed with work. No matter what your level of skill is when it comes to VBA there is always room to learn more. By following these basic guidelines, you are less likely to get sidetracked by common errors that could zap your enthusiasm for writing code. You will be able to stay focused and completely tuned to everything you are learning and as a result, your ability to write code will be a more enjoyable experience in the long run.

THE CHEAT SHEET FOR EXCEL FORMULAS

You can use Excel to prepare reports, perform calculations, create text-based files, and much more. Many people have used this program to accomplish great things. In this cheat sheet, you'll find the formulas that you need to complete your tasks with Excel.

The Most Popular Functions

Some functions have certain requirements. Most functions, however, apply to any situation. Here are the functions that you will likely use in Excel 2016:

IF – This function tests a condition. It will give you a value depending on the result of the test.

INT – This function deletes the decimal part of numeric values. Thus, you will turn your numbers into integers.

NOW – Use this function to get the current time and date values of your computer.

SUM – With this function, you can get the total of a set of values.

ROUND – This function can round numbers to specific digit positions or decimal places.

COUNT – Use this function to count the cells that hold numbers.

SUMIF – This is the combination of SUM and IF. It will give you the total of the values that satisfy your predetermined conditions.

TODAY – This function will give you the current date value of your system.

AVERAGE – With this function, you can get the average of a set of values.

COUNTIF – This function is the combination of IF and COUNT. It counts cells that meet your criteria.

The Text Functions that You Should Use

Excel 2016 has functions that work on text-based data (e.g. names, phone numbers, email addresses). The list given below will describe how text functions work:

LEN – Use this function to count the characters inside your chosen cell/range.

MID – This function can extract characters. It allows you to specify the number of characters to be extracted and the starting point of the process.

LEFT – This function extracts characters starting from the first character of the text.

RIGHT – With this function, you can extract characters starting from the final character of the text.

UPPER – Use this function to convert letters to uppercase.

LOWER – Use this function to convert letters to lowercase.

REPLACE – This function replaces text with another text.

PROPER – With this function, you can capitalize the first character of each word.

CONCATENATE – Use this function to combine two or more text strings.

The Operation Precedence in Excel 2016

Mathematical operations follow a particular order, and the Excel program follows that order. The list you'll find below describes the order that Excel and math operations follow:

- Operations inside parentheses
- Operations that involve exponents
- Multiplication
- Division
- Addition
- Subtraction

The Cell References in Excel 2016

You can use relative or absolute cell references in your Excel formulas. When you are copying a formula to other cells, the things that you'll need to modify depend on the kind of reference you are using. The formula may adjust its references automatically so that it matches the new cell (i.e. for relative references). It's also possible that the reference will point to the same cell regardless of the formula's new location (i.e. for absolute references).

Excel lets you combine absolute and relative references in your formulas. Thus, you can make formulas that have fixed rows and adjustable columns, or fixed columns and adjustable rows.

In Excel 2016, you can set a reference as absolute by placing a dollar symbol. Here are some examples:

> **D1** – This reference is completely relative.
>
> **D$1** – This reference has a relative row and absolute column.
>
> **$D1** – This reference has an absolute row and relative column.
>
> **$D$1** – This reference is completely absolute.

The Error Messages in Excel 2016

Excel is capable of displaying error messages. Thus, you'll immediately know whenever you make a mistake. Error messages usually appear whenever you create a circular reference or a formula that has incorrect elements. Knowing what an error value means is the first step in solving formula-related problems.

Here are the error values that you'll encounter while using Excel 2016:

#N/A – One of your functions or formulas cannot find your referenced information.

#NULL! - This value states that you used a space in a multi-range reference. You should use commas to separate ranges.

#REF! - You used an invalid reference.

#DIV/0 – You are attempting to divide a value by zero.

#VALUE – You assigned the wrong kind of argument to your function or formula.

#NAME? - Excel doesn't recognize the text or name inside your formula.

#NUM! - You used an invalid number in your formula.

SOME OTHER TIPS ON VBA PROGRAMMING

Other than the tools mentioned earlier and some tips mentioned along the way earlier, below are some other tips on VBA programming for beginners.

Writing more efficient VBA code

Working with arrays instead of a range of cells

Let us compare the execution times between these two approaches. Suppose you want to count the number of numbers that are divisible by four in a range of 50,000 cells. The code that works with an array is generally faster than the one switches between VBA and Excel. The following table shows the execution times (in seconds) for two different approaches in counting the number of numbers that are divisible by four in a range of 50,000 cells:

Working with a range of cells	Working with an array
0.20	0.031

The listing below is an example of VBA code that works with a range of cells.

```vba
Sub WorkingWithRange()
    'To count the number of numbers that are
    'divisible by 4 in a range of 50,000 cells.
    Dim r As Long, c As Long
    Dim rN As Long, cN As Long
    Dim cnt As Long
    Dim StartTimer As Date, EndTimer As Date
    StartTimer = Timer
    rN = 500:  cN = 100:  cnt = 0
    For r = 1 To rN
        For c = 1 To cN
            If Sheets(1).Cells(r, c) Mod 4 = 0 _
            Then cnt = cnt + 1
        Next c
    Next r
    EndTimer = Timer
    Debug.Print cnt
    Debug.Print EndTimer - StartTimer
```

End Sub

Another listing is an example of much faster VBA code that works with an array.

```vba
Sub WorkingWithAnArray()
    'To count the number of numbers that are
    'divisible by 4 in a range of 50,000 cells.
    Dim x() As Variant
    Dim r As Long, c As Long
    Dim rN As Long, cN As Long
    Dim cnt As Long
    Dim StartTimer As Date, EndTimer As Date
    StartTimer = Timer
    rN = 500:  cN = 100:  cnt = 0
    ReDim x(rN, cN)
    Sheets(1).Activate
    x = Range("A1").Resize(rN, cN)
    For r = 1 To rN
        For c = 1 To cN
            If x(r, c) Mod 4 = 0 Then _
                cnt = cnt + 1
```

```
        Next c

    Next r

    EndTimer = Timer

    Debug.Print cnt

    Debug.Print EndTimer - StartTimer
End Sub
```

Disabling screen updating, alert displays, events, and automatic calculations

If they are not necessary during the execution of your VBA code, disable them before the execution and restore them to their initial settings right before the execution ends. Restoring the settings rather than turning them all on is a good practice since some users may have different settings, as shown in the following listing.

```
'Declaration
Dim ScrnU As Boolean, DispA As Boolean, _
Evnt As Boolean, Calc As Long
'Save the settings
With Application
        ScrnU = .ScreenUpdating
        DispA = .DisplayAlerts
```

```
        Evnt = .EnableEvents
        Calc = .Calculation
End With
'Disable them before the execution begins
With Application
        .ScreenUpdating = False
        .DisplayAlerts = False
        .EnableEvents = False
        .Calculation = xlCalculationManual
End With
 'Here runs your code
'Restore the initial settings
'before the execution ends
With Application
        .ScreenUpdating = ScrnU
        .DisplayAlerts = DispA
        .EnableEvents = Evnt
        .Calculation = Calc
End With
```

The above VBA code can be improved by removing the need of saving and restoring the ScreenUpdating and DisplayAlerts properties. As I was writing this manuscript, these properties were reset to True when the code execution ended. Nevertheless, as a matter of practice you may want explicitly to set their properties back to True when the procedure ends, as shown below:

'Declaration

Dim Evnt As Boolean, Calc As Long

'Save the settings

With Application

    Evnt = .EnableEvents

    Calc = .Calculation

End With

'Disable them before the execution begins

With Application

    .ScreenUpdating = False

    .DisplayAlerts = False

    .EnableEvents = False

    .Calculation = xlCalculationManual

End With

'Here runs your code

'Restore the default and initial settings

'before the execution ends

With Application

    .ScreenUpdating = True

    .DisplayAlerts = True

    .EnableEvents = Evnt

    .Calculation = Calc

End With

Reducing the size of a working range

Reduce the size of a working range whenever possible.

Let us take a fictitious situation to discuss this. Suppose that you have written the following SumSelectedRange1 procedure to sum up all the numbers in a selected range of cells.

Sub SumSelectedRange1()

'To sum numbers in a selected range

Dim cel As Range, sum As Double

    If TypeName(Selection) <> "Range" Then

        MsgBox "Please select a range."

    Exit Sub

End If

For Each cel In Selection

    If VBA.IsNumeric(cel) Then _

        sum = sum + cel

Next cel

MsgBox "The sum of all the numbers in " & _ "the selected range is " & Sum

End Sub

If a user selects an entire sheet of cells, the above procedure will take a very long time to complete its execution because it is actually processing 17,179,869,184 cells. The above procedure can be improved by considering only used range of cells in the worksheet, as shown in the following listing.

Sub SumSelectedRange2()

'To sum numbers in a selected range

'In case a user selected an entire row,

'column, or sheet

Dim cel As Range, sum As Double

Dim WorkRng As Range

    If TypeName(Selection) <> "Range" Then

        MsgBox "Please select a range."

```
        Exit Sub

End If

Set WorkRng = Intersect(Selection,ActiveSheet.UsedRange)

For Each cel In WorkRng

If VBA.IsNumeric(cel) Then _

sum = sum + cel

Next cel

MsgBox "The sum of all the numbers in " & _

"the selected range is " & Sum

End Sub
```

The ActiveSheet.UsedRange property returns the range of cells that are used in the active worksheet. Hence, the SumSelectedRange2 procedure has greatly reduced the number of cells to be processed.

However, the UsedRange property of the Worksheet object does not actually determine the cells that have really been used. To understand what I meant, execute the following steps:

1. Start a blank workbook.
2. Enter something (a number or text) into cell A1 in a worksheet.

3. Press Ctrl+↓ (the down-arrow key) to reach the last cell in column A, that is, cell A1048576.
4. Press Ctrl+→ (the right-arrow key) to reach the rightmost bottom cell in the worksheet, that is, cell XFD1048576.
5. Enter something (a number or text) into this cell XFD1048576.
6. Press Alt+F11 to activate VBE.
7. In the Immediate window, enter the following statement:

ActiveSheet.UsedRange.Address

It returns $1:$1048576, that is, the address of the entire cells in the worksheet.

If the SumSelectedRange2 procedure is executed for a worksheet where cell A1 and cell XFD1048576 are used, then there is no difference in term of execution between SumSelectedRange1 and SumSelectedRange2 (if the entire worksheet selected by a user before execution). Nevertheless, in very rare cases, only cell A1 (or any cells near cell A1) and cell XFD1048576 (or any cells near the last column XFD and the last row 1048576) are used, but in between these cells mostly unused.

Another way to improve the execution time of SumSelectedRange1 is to deal with only those cells with numbers. VBA provides a quick way to identify those cells: the SpecialCells method, as shown in the SumSelectedRange3 procedure below.

```
Sub SumSelectedRange3()
    'To sum numbers in a selected range
    'Only working with numbers
    Dim cel As Range, sum As Double
    Dim ConstantNumbers As Range, FormulaNumbers As Range
    If TypeName(Selection) <> "Range" Then
        MsgBox "Please select a range."
        Exit Sub
    End If
On Error Resume Next  'if no cells were found
Set ConstantNumbers = Selection. _
SpecialCells(xlConstants, 1)
Set FormulaNumbers = Selection. _
SpecialCells(xlFormulas, 1)
On Error GoTo 0
'Sum constant numbers
If Not ConstantNumbers Is Nothing Then
    For Each cel In ConstantNumbers
        sum = sum + cel
```

```
        Next cel
    End If
    'Sum numbers in formula cells
    If Not FormulaNumbers Is Nothing Then
        For Each cel In FormulaNumbers
            sum = sum + cel
        Next cel
    End If
        MsgBox "The sum of all the numbers in " & _
    "the selected range is " & Sum
    End Sub
```

SEARCH AND REFERENCE FORMULAS

Now is the time to talk about one of the most important formulas in Excel, the Search and Reference formulas. In order to become and Excel Formulas Champion you need to master at least 2 formulas in this segment.

These formulas are widely used because of their ability to save time with databases. The 3 formulas that we are going to explore are:

- VLOOKUP
- HLOOKUP
- XLOOKUP

Let's start!

VLOOKUP FUNCTION

WHAT IS THIS FUNCTION FOR?

To make this simple, this formula is the most used in Excel. It is used to obtain values (related to a reference cell) from a big database without having to find them manually.

WHICH IS THE MAIN BENEFIT OF THIS FORMULA?

You can easily find and relate info from a database in order to match the info that you are looking for. You'll understand it better with the exercise.

HOW IS THIS FUNCTION STRUCTURED?

The syntax (Structure) of the VLOOKUP function is another one:

=VLOOKUP(lookup value, lookup array, column, range lookup)

WHAT DOES THAT MEAN?

LOOKUP VALUE: Is the base Value that you already know. Excel will try to find that value in a database and return another value (in another column) that matches your lookup value

LOOKUP ARRAY: Is the range where the data base is located

COLUMN: Is the Column number (of the database) where your desired result is located. If you want to get the result from the 2nd column in the database, you will need to write 2 in this argument.

RANGE LOOKUP: This is optional, normally you want to use "0" because that means you want an EXACT MATCH. This way Excel will only find values that match exactly with your LOOKUP VALUE.

Let's try an exercise for you to understand it better.

EXERCISE

Now you have an ID search cell and some info that you need to pull out of a database. To your right you have a big data base with the information in random order.

ID	HEROE	SECTOR	CITY
1	The Atom	Healthcare	Danvers, Massachusetts
2	X-Men	Utilities	Canonsburg, Pennsylvania
3	Asterix	Industrial Goods	North Chicago, Illinois

DATA BASE

Due to the COVID crisis, with no wars and no violence, our heroes needed to start working in some companies (although it was hard for them to get a job). Each one of them has an ID assigned. We need to build a tool to search the whole information by just changing the ID.

14	
22	
56	

SEARCH TOOL

IMPORTANT NOTE:

Notice that we have 1 piece of information that matches in our Search Tool and in our Database. That piece of information is the ID NUMBER, so what we need to do is to use that ID NUMBER as an ANCHOR value (Lookup Value) to grab the other values that we need (The name of the hero)

Step 1: Please start writing the formula at B3, to get the first hero name.

=VLOOKUP(

Step 2: The 1st argument (The lookup value) is our "anchor value", the value that we have in both tables, the ID NUMBER. So select the corresponding cell. In this case is first the cell with an ID number in our search tool, A3

=VLOOKUP(A3,

Why? Because Excel will try to find in the database whatever we have in A3 (in this case, excel will try to find in the database the number 14)

Step 3: Select the Lookup Array (The database) in order to indicate excel where to search. Remember to add ABSOLUTE REFERENCES in order to be able to drag the formula eventually.

=VLOOKUP(A3,$F$2:$J$89,

Why? Because the database starts in F2 and ends in J89.

SUPER IMPORTANT NOTE:

IN ORDER FOR VLOOKUP TO WORK CORRECTLY, THE FIRST COLUMN IN THE DATABASE MUST HAVE YOUR LOOKUP VALUE (ANCHOR VALUE). IN OTHER WORDS, IF YOU ARE USING THE ID NUMBER AS YOUR LOOKUP VALUE, THE ID NUMBER MUST BE IN THE FIRST COLUMN (LEFT COLUMN) OF YOUR DATABASE.

Step 3: Write the column number where your desired result is. In this example, your desired result is the name of the hero, so, IN YOUR DATABASE the name of the hero is in the 2nd Column, then you need to write 2.

=VLOOKUP(A3,$F$2:$J$89,2

Step 3: Write 0, in order to get and EXACT search. Close and drag the formula.

=VLOOKUP(A3,$F$2:$J$89,2,0)

14	Optimus Prime
2	Catwoman
56	Fantastic Four
70	Rocky Balboa

80	Gandalf

That's it! Look how fast you got the names of the heroes using their IDs, and if you change the ID number the name will change too! Try it.

20	Zorro
30	Doc Savage
40	Luke Skywalker

Now try by yourself to fill the search tool completely!

14	Optimus Prime		
22	Catwoman		
56	Fantastic Four		
70	Rocky Balboa		
80	Gandalf		

DEPARTMENT DATA VALIDATION

We want to allow a user to enter a department number and have Excel automatically populate the related department name. The result is illustrated in Figure 14 below.

⬤ PRACTICE

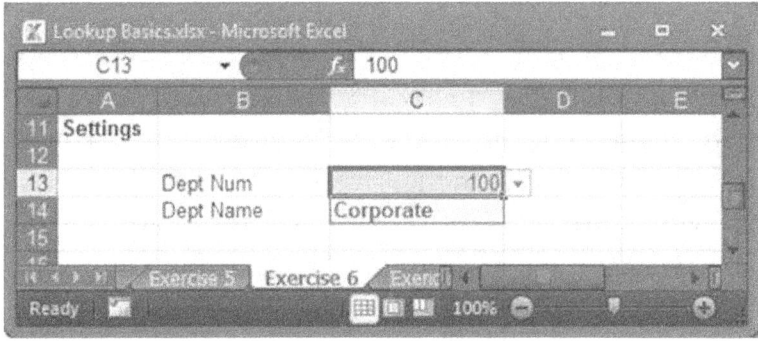

Figure 14

Summary

If we think about the goal for a minute, we can piece together the Excel items needed. Here we'll discuss the features and functions required at a summary level, and in the Step-by-Step unit below we'll chronologically work through the detailed steps.

We allow the user to enter a department number into the input cell and then use the VLOOKUP function to retrieve the proper department name.

Since we are asking Excel to perform a lookup, we'll need to store the department list somewhere inside the workbook. Since we want the user's experience to be clean, we place the department list on a separate worksheet. Since we may ultimately add more departments over time, we choose to store the department list in a table named tbl_depts.

Since we want to be clear about which cell requires input, we identify the input cell with the Input cell style.

Since our lookup formula is designed to return the name for the departments appearing in our list, it would return an error if the user entered a department number that wasn't in the list. To prevent this error, we provide a drop-down to restrict input to a list of valid department numbers with the data validation feature.

Since data validation does not directly support structured table references, we must first set up the custom name dd_depts, which refers to the structured table reference for the department number column.

Here is a summary of the independent Excel items mentioned above:

A table stores the department list.

The named reference enables the drop-down list to use the table data.

The Input cell style highlights the input cell.

The data validation feature provides the in-cell drop-down.

The VLOOKUP function retrieves the department name.

Good times! Now that we have worked through the overall concepts, let's sort through the specifics.

Step-by-Step

Here are the steps to setting up the worksheet.

DEPENDS ON

Step 1: Table. Since we use the workbook on a recurring basis and want to make it easy to add new departments, we convert the ordinary range of departments found on the Exercise 6 Data sheet to a table named tbl_depts.

NOTE

My personal preference is to start table names with tbl_.

Step 2: Named range. We need to set up a name that refers to the table's department number column so that we can use it with the data validation feature. We assign the name dd_depts to the department number column of the table tbl_depts[Dept Num].

NOTE

My personal preference is to start names that are used to provide a drop-down list with dd_.

Step 3: Input cell style. We want to make it easy for the user to identify which cell requires input, so we apply the Input cell style to the input cell.

Step 4: Data validation. We create an in-cell drop-down in the input cell by setting up data validation to allow a list equal to our name dd_depts.

Step 5: Lookup formula. After the user picks a valid department number from the drop-down list in C13, we ask Excel to display the corresponding department name with the following lookup function:

=VLOOKUP(C13,tbl_depts,2,0)

Where:

C13 is the value we are looking up, the department number.

tbl_depts is the lookup range, the table of departments.

2 is the column that has the value we wish to return, the department name column.

0 means we are not doing a range lookup.

Wow, wasn't that a rush? Using five independent Excel features and functions in harmony to achieve a goal—so fun!

This specific combination of features and functions is quite handy. Once comfortable coordinating the individual steps, you'll quickly be able to use this approach in your workbooks.

BALANCE SHEET LOOKUP

In this exercise we'll build a financial statement from an export from our accounting system. We'll set up the workbook so that each period when we paste in updated data, Excel automatically recalculates the financial statement amounts. Each period, we just paste and go; that's hands-free reporting.

◉ PRACTICE

To work along, please reference the Exercise 7 worksheet.

Let's pretend that periodically we obtain an extract from our accounting system that reflects each account's current balance. For simplicity, we'll refer to our export as the trial balance. Let's also pretend we want Excel to automatically place the values found in the trial balance into a perfectly formatted financial statement.

The overall idea is simple: create one worksheet in the workbook dedicated to storing the trial balance, and then set up the financial statement using lookup formulas that pull the right values into the right cells in the report. Since the report values are generated by formulas, they will automatically refresh as soon as an updated trial balance is pasted into the workbook.

You've already written many VLOOKUP functions, so this should be pretty easy. I did add one little twist, which demonstrates how to use column-only references with a lookup formula.

NOTE

How can we ensure that all data in the trial balance flows properly through to the financial statement? With an ErrorCk sheet, of course.

XREF

Take a look at the Exercise 7 Data sheet to observe the exported data. These are the values we'll ultimately pull into the Exercise 7 sheet, which represents the balance sheet. We'll use the VLOOKUP function to retrieve the values.

We want to write our balance sheet formulas so that they include any new rows that may appear in the trial balance over time. My preferred method is to store the trial balance in a table. Since this isn't always an available option or is sometimes not appropriate, let's explore an alternative method: column-only references.

A column-only reference, such as B:B, includes the entire column. If the following month's data occupies more rows than last month, using a column-only reference as an argument ensures the function will include all data.

XREF

Column-only references are introduced earlier. This exercise illustrates a practical application of them.

The lookup formula used to pull the values from the trial balance into the balance sheet follows:

=VLOOKUP(B14,'Exercise 7 Data'!B:C,2,0)

Where:

B14 is the value we are looking up, the account name.

'Exercise 7 Data'!B:C is the lookup range, the exported data on the Exercise 7 Data sheet; note the column-only reference B:C.

2 is the column that contains the value we want to return, the amount.

0 means we are not doing a range lookup.

 KB

Here are the steps to writing the formula using only your keyboard. Type =VL, and then hit Tab to insert the VLOOKUP function from the auto-complete list into the cell. Left Arrow twice to insert the B14 cell reference into the first function argument. Type a comma to finish the first argument. Use Ctrl+PageDown to switch to the Exercise 7 Data sheet. Use the arrow keys to navigate to any cell in column B. Hit Ctrl+Space to select the entire column. Hold down Shift and then press the Right Arrow to extend your selection to include column C as well. Type a comma to finish the second argument. Type a 2 as the third argument, and then a comma. Type 0, close the parenthesis, and then press Enter.

The results are shown in the partial balance sheet in Figure 15 below.

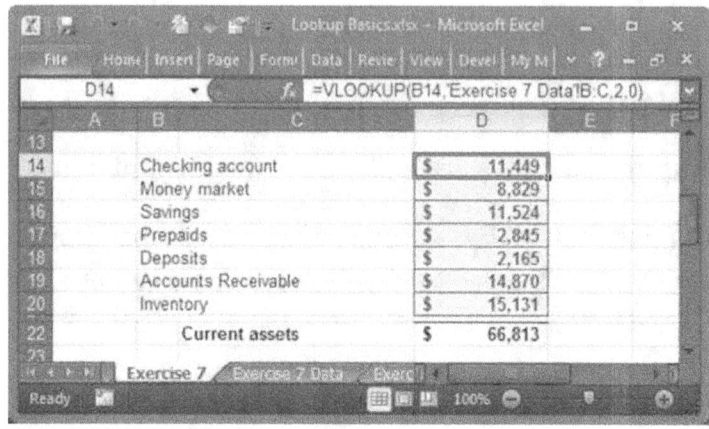

Figure 15

 **XREF**

Please note that this exercise worksheet relies on the SUBTOTAL function for adding and utilizes skinny rows.

Since the report was built with formulas, when we paste in the updated trial balance the following month, the balance sheet amounts refresh automagically!

TRICK QUESTIONS

Okay, time for a quick intermission between our hands-on exercises. I'd like to ask you some trick questions about the VLOOKUP function.

Question #1: Where does it look?

When the VLOOKUP function is trying to find the matching value in the lookup range (as specified by the second argument), where within that range is it actually looking? I'll give you two choices: it looks in all cells of the lookup range, or it looks only in the first column. What do you think?

Answer: The VLOOKUP function looks for a matching value in the first column of the lookup range—that is, the left-most column within the range defined by the second argument. After a match is found, the VLOOKUP then uses the other columns in the range to return its result. But the original match is performed within the first column only.

Question #2: Does the column number specified in the third argument refer to the absolute worksheet column or the relative column within the lookup range?

The third argument of the VLOOKUP function indicates which column has the value we want to return. This argument is specified as a column index number, such as 5, 7, or 9. So the question is whether the column index number refers to the absolute worksheet column—such as column B = 2 and column E = 5—or does it refer to the relative column within the lookup range, as defined in the second argument? What do you think?

Answer: The column number refers to the relative column within the lookup range. So if the amount column is the second column within the lookup range, but happens to be in column E, we would use a value of 2.

Question #3: What happens if a matching value can't be found?

If the function tries to find a matching value, but a matching value can't be found in the first column of the lookup range, what happens? I'll give you two choices: Excel returns an error code, or Excel returns the closest match. What do you think?

Answer: It depends on the value of the fourth argument. If the fourth argument is FALSE, then the function returns the error code #N/A when a matching value is not found. If the fourth argument is TRUE, then it returns the closest match based on the function's range lookup logic.

The range lookup logic tells the function to search row by row, one at a time, in order, until it finds a row that contains a value that is less than the lookup value and where the following row is greater than the lookup value. At this point, the function stops looking and returns the related value. According to the Excel help file, "The following largest value that is less than lookup_value is returned." This logic is, admittedly, very confusing. It reminds me of the show The Price is Right, where the contestants need to guess the highest price without going over. It is easier to make sense of this logic when applied in an actual worksheet, so we'll do some additional exercises shortly that will help.

THE OBJECT MODEL

1: Classes and Objects

Just as with problem solving, there are various paradigms that can be used to help think about programming in an organized way. Up until the early 1990's, the most popular approach was top-down stepwise refinement. In this method, we start by thinking about the task we want our program to do. That task is broken down into subtasks, and those are broken down in turn, until finally we have a task small enough to be programmed easily. These small pieces can be individually tested and assembled into ever larger chunks until finally you have a finished piece of software that can accomplish the original task.

This approach works pretty well but it has one significant flaw. The small procedures that are developed tend to be quite specialized for whatever the context of the problem is, and not readily adaptable for use in other programs. For each piece of software, you have to start over from the beginning, even if you've written programs that do very similar tasks.

The newer model that has been widely adopted and is currently popular is almost the polar opposite of the top-down approach. In this method, called object-oriented programming, you start by thinking about the "objects" your program needs to manipulate. They could be things like elements of the user interface, files, worksheets, or anything else that is part of the universe of items available to your program. Each category of objects has its own characteristics: properties that you might want the program to change, sub-objects that it can contain, actions that it can take (or that can be carried out on it), and events you would like it respond to. A category of objects is called a class. Essentially, you begin your work by determining the classes of objects you'll use, and either writing code for them to carry out all the needed operations, or, if you're lucky, using a class of objects that someone else has already developed.

This approach leads to robust, reusable code, in the form of a library of classes. Most programs use the same kinds of objects, and so a lot of effort can be put into developing a class with the knowledge that the work will pay off in the future on other projects. Having a nice library of well-written classes means that programming is much easier and can avoid a lot of the low-level detail involved in things like changing a font or a color. In VBA, there is a huge universe of classes to choose from. All the required elements are provided and you just need to write the code that manipulates them.

The distinction between a class and an object is a bit subtle. A class of objects is like a framework or pattern that describes the objects that belong to the class. An object is an instance of its class. A real-world example would be the class of chairs. There is a general concept of chairs, which we could compare to a class. And then there are actual chairs, each of which is an instance of the class.

Classes and objects form a hierarchy. In VBA, the Application is at the topmost level of the hierarchy; if you're working in Excel, the Application is Excel itself. (There are versions of VBA embedded in many other Microsoft products, with classes designed for their individual applications, though there is often quite a bit of overlap.) Excel itself contains other objects, most prominently Workbooks. Workbooks contain Worksheets, Charts, and other kinds of things; Worksheets contain Ranges. (A Cell is a special kind of Range.) Often an object can contain not just one but a whole collection of sub-objects of a given type. So Workbooks can contain many Worksheets and Charts; a Worksheet can contain many Ranges.

To appeal to a real-world analogy, think of the Application as being like a house. A house can include many kinds of objects such as a roof, a front porch, a back yard, etc., but mainly we would focus on rooms. A room can contain lots of kinds of things, one of which is chairs. A dining room probably has many chairs. It may have a cabinet that contains dishes. So there is a hierarchy of a house and its contents. Each class of objects has its own properties and things that it's used for and possibly other objects it contains. You can't push an analogy like this too far, but I hope it gives you a feeling for what the hierarchy is like.

Now, let's look at a specific example. In Excel, we have a ListBox class. Every actual ListBox is an object in this class. It has properties such as Left (horizontal position of upper left corner), Height, Visible, and others. It has methods, such as AddItem and Clear. And it has events for which there are built-in functions.

> Open a project in the VBA editor and create a text box. Take a look at the various properties. Try setting some to see what happens.

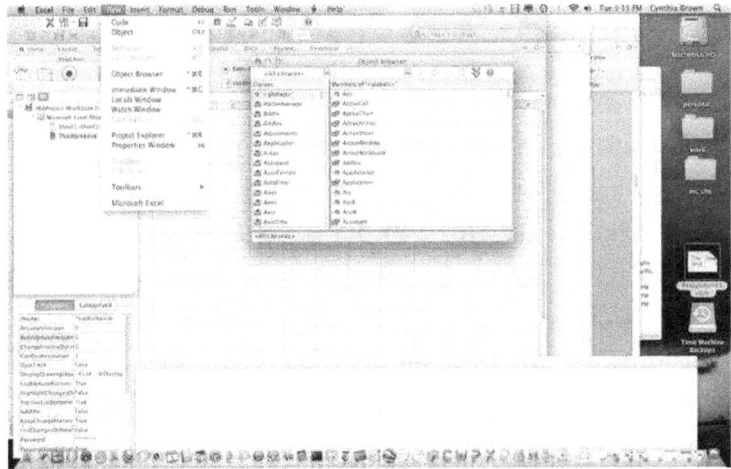

Figure 8-1 The Object Browser (under the View menu)

To get a look at all the methods, properties, and events for the class ListBox, we can use the object browser. This is a feature of VBA that lets you explore the object hierarchy and find out what you can do with various classes of objects. The figure shows the object browser featuring a view of ListBox. The object browser is under the View menu.

Note the small icons distinguishing properties, methods, and events. We've highlighted the Locked property; it's a property with a Boolean value that can be set in code or in the Properties window. A note at the bottom tells us that ListBox is a member of class MSForms; listboxes appear in many applications, not just Excel.

> Go into the object browser and look up ListBox. You do that by searching for it in All Libraries (see the top of the Figure). Click on ListBox to see the list of its members. Go through the list and see if there are any useful members you

2: Names and References

VBA makes extensive use of the dot (.) to construct names and navigate the object hierarchy. Suppose I have a Workbook called IndexListBox containing a form called frmIndexListBox, and that the form contains a ListBox called lstWord. Now, suppose I want to refer to this ListBox in my code. Of course, we've already done this! But we did so under the assumption that the Workbook and form are active at the time the code is running. By default, VBA expects names to refer to objects contained in active objects, and in that case we can just use the name itself, and the meaning is clear.

But suppose for some reason I am writing some code for the IndexListBox workbook, and I want to refer to lstWord while the form is not active. In that case I use a fuller version of the name, frmIndexListBox.lstWord. And if necessary I can refer to a form in a Workbook that is not active, using IndexListBox.frmIndexListBox.lstWord. Normally there is not much reason to refer to members of inactive objects, but this shows you how to do it in principle. Alternatively, you can activate objects like Workbooks and forms in your code using their Activate methods.

In general, the complete name of an object starts with the top of the hierarchy (Application) and works its way down, with a dot separating each level. But again, you don't need to bother with this if you know that the containing object will be active when you need to refer to it.

The last item in a list of names separated by dots can be the name of an object, but often it is the name of a method or property instead. For example, to invoke the AddItem method with ListBox lstWord, we would write something like lstWord.AddItem("crimson"). Or we might use Cells(1,2).Value to refer to the contents of Cell B1.

If you type the name of an object and then a dot, VBA will typically show you all the possible completions that can follow the dot. This is a very useful feature. If you remember the beginning of the name of a member, but not the whole name, type the first couple of letters and VBA will show you the choices with that prefix. And, of course, you can always use the object browser to see what's available.

Summary

Programming Practices

Think in terms of objects when designing your program. In VBA, especially, there is a rich library of objects to take advantage of. Don't reinvent the wheel if you don't have to

If you often have to write code to complete similar tasks, consider developing objects, or at least reusable pieces of code that can be the basis for your programs

Important Terms

Object: an entity realized in software that a program can manipulate

Object-oriented programming: a programming paradigm in which the code is built using operations on objects

Class: A category of objects that have the same properties, methods, and events; a template for an object in the category

Instance: an object is an instance of its class

Object browser: a feature in VBA that shows you the object hierarchy and the members of each class; very useful when you are wondering how to carry out some procedure on or with an object

RELATIVE AND ABSOLUTE REFERENCES

If we copy and paste a VLOOKUP function from one cell into another cell, and we do not specify that the referenced value is absolute, Excel assumes our reference is relative. It thinks we are in the car together, but, in actuality, we dropped our reference off at the rest area. Essentially, it went to use the bathroom, and I left.

Chicken and Egg

To illustrate this, we will first look at the Chicken Egg worksheet.

The goal here is to copy everything from cells A2 through B4 into cells D2 through E4 while using VLOOKUP.

When we enter the following formula into cell D2, everything matches up the way we expect:

=VLOOKUP(A2,A2:B3,1,0)

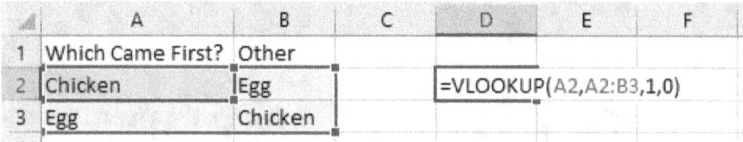

Figure 37: The Chicken Egg worksheet with an effective VLOOKUP formula

If we copy that formula and paste it into cell E2, the formula will read:

=VLOOKUP(B2,B2:C3,1,0)

The result may be what was expected, but look at what VLOOKUP selected for the lookup value and table array:

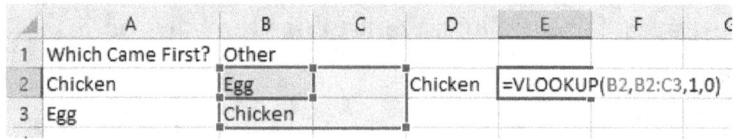

Figure 38: The Chicken Egg table with a VLOOKUP formula that has been mislaid

The lookup value is B2, which shifted one cell to the right from when my formula was in cell D2. My table array also shifted one cell to the right – from A2:B3 to B2:C3. All of these references are relative.

Let's see what happens when we change one reference to be absolute.

First, delete the contents of cells D2 and E2. Then type the following into D2:

=VLOOKUP($A2,A2:B3,1,0)

Now copy and paste that into cell E2. The result is Chicken, but why?

Look at where the lookup value is pointing:

	A	B	C	D	E	F	G
1	Which Came First?	Other					
2	Chicken	Egg			Chicken	=VLOOKUP($A2,B2:C3,1,0)	
3	Egg	Chicken					

Figure 39: With an absolute column reference, the lookup value is now correct

The dollar sign ($) makes the reference to column A absolute, so when we copy and paste the formula into cell E2, the lookup value is still pointing to Chicken in cell A2.

What happens when this spans over several values, and how do we ensure it is set up correctly? We will explore another example to answer those questions.

Rock, Paper, Scissors

To see this happen with more detail, go to the Rock Paper Scissors worksheet.

Once again, we will try to copy the contents of cells A1 through D4 and paste them into cells G2 through I4, using VLOOKUP.

In cell B2, type:

=VLOOKUP(A2,F1:I4,2,0)

Now select and copy this cell, then paste it into cell C2. Does everything look like it should?

When we select cell B2, we see in the formula that:

Ref1 is our lookup value

The table at the right is our table array

The column index is 2

The range is 0

	A	B	C	D	E	F	G	H	I
1	Lookup Value	Item 1	Item 2	Item 3		Lookup Value	Item 1	Item 2	Item 3
2	Ref1	=VLOOKUP(A2,F1:I4,2,0)				Ref1	rock	paper	scissors
3	Ref2					Ref2	rock	scissors	chicken nuggets
4	Ref3					Ref3	scissors	rock	candy bar
5			2	3	4				

Figure 40: The Rock Paper Scissors worksheet with an effective VLOOKUP formula in cell B2

Compare that with what happens when we select cell C2. We see:

Rock is our lookup value

The table array excludes column F and includes the empty column J

The column index is still 2, but should it be?

The range is 0

	A	B	C	D	E	F	G	H	I	J
1	Lookup Value	Item 1	Item 2	Item 3		Lookup Value	Item 1	Item 2	Item 3	
2	Ref1	rock	=VLOOKUP(B2,G1:J4,2,0)			Ref1	rock	paper	scissors	
3	Ref2					Ref2	rock	scissors	chicken nuggets	
4	Ref3					Ref3	scissors	rock	candy bar	
5			2	3	4					

Figure 41: The Rock Paper Scissors worksheet with a misaligned formula in cell C2

So, what went wrong? We told Excel that all the cell references are relative, but some of them need to be absolute.

We will continue to look at how information shifts when using relative references, then we will address how to solve it.

Select and copy cell B2, then select cells B2 through D4 and paste – simultaneously filling all nine cells with the formula. What did you get?

Do cells B2 through D4 match what is in cells G2 through I4? If they do match, then you did not enter the preceding formula precisely. The cell references will shift depending on the cell and, therefore, will result in different values. The following illustrations demonstrate this.

Cell B2 contains our original formula:

=VLOOKUP(A2,F1:I4,2,0)

	A	B	C	D	E	F	G	H	I
1	Lookup Value	Item 1	Item 2	Item 3		Lookup Value	Item 1	Item 2	Item 3
2	Ref1	=VLOOKUP(A2,F1:I4,2,0)				Ref1	rock	paper	scissors
3	Ref2	rock	paper	scissors		Ref2	rock	scissors	chicken nuggets
4	Ref3	scissors	rock	candy bar		Ref3	scissors	rock	candy bar
5			2	3	4				

Figure 42: Our original formula

In cell C2, we see the cells in the formula are shifted one place to the right:

=VLOOKUP(B2,G1:J4,2,0)

	A	B	C	D	E	F	G	H	I	J
1	Lookup Value	Item 1	Item 2	Item 3		Lookup Value	Item 1	Item 2	Item 3	
2	Ref1	rock	=VLOOKUP(B2,G1:J4,2,0)			Ref1	rock	paper	scissors	
3	Ref2	rock	paper	scissors		Ref2	rock	scissors	chicken nuggets	
4	Ref3	scissors	rock	candy bar		Ref3	scissors	rock	candy bar	
5			2	3	4					

Figure 43: The formula pasted one cell to the right has misplaced arguments

In cell D2, the cells in the formula are shifted one more cell to the right:

=VLOOKUP(C2,H1:K4,2,0)

	A	B	C	D	E	F	G	H	I	J	K
1	Lookup Value	Item 1	Item 2	Item 3		Lookup Value	Item 1	Item 2	Item 3		
2	Ref1	rock	paper	=VLOOKUP(C2,H1:K4,2,0)		Ref1	rock	paper	scissors		
3	Ref2	rock	paper	scissors		Ref2	rock	scissors	chicken nuggets		
4	Ref3	scissors	rock	candy bar		Ref3	scissors	rock	candy bar		
5				2	3	4					

Figure 44: In the adjacent cell to the right, the arguments have shifted again

If we look at the cells beneath B2, we will see a similar behavior.

Once again, for reference, this is cell B2 with our original formula:

=VLOOKUP(A2,F1:I4,2,0)

	A	B	C	D	E	F	G	H	I
1	Lookup Value	Item 1	Item 2	Item 3		Lookup Value	Item 1	Item 2	Item 3
2	Ref1	=VLOOKUP(A2,F1:I4,2,0)				Ref1	rock	paper	scissors
3	Ref2	rock	paper	scissors		Ref2	rock	scissors	chicken nuggets
4	Ref3	scissors	rock	candy bar		Ref3	scissors	rock	candy bar
5			2	3	4				

Figure 45: Our original formula

In cell B3, the columns remain constant in the formula, but the row numbers shift:

=VLOOKUP(A3,F2:I5,2,0)

	A	B	C	D	E	F	G	H	I
1	Lookup Value	Item 1	Item 2	Item 3		Lookup Value	Item 1	Item 2	Item 3
2	Ref1	rock	paper	scissors		Ref1	rock	paper	scissors
3	Ref2	=VLOOKUP(A3,F2:I5,2,0)				Ref2	rock	scissors	chicken nuggets
4	Ref3	scissors	rock	candy bar		Ref3	scissors	rock	candy bar
5		2	3	4					

Figure 46: The formula pasted in the row below has arguments that are also down one row

In cell B4, we see the row numbers have shifted again:

=VLOOKUP(A4,F3:I6,2,0)

	A	B	C	D	E	F	G	H	I
1	Lookup Value	Item 1	Item 2	Item 3		Lookup Value	Item 1	Item 2	Item 3
2	Ref1	rock	paper	scissors		Ref1	rock	paper	scissors
3	Ref2	rock	paper	scissors		Ref2	rock	scissors	chicken nuggets
4	Ref3	=VLOOKUP(A4,F3:I6,2,0)				Ref3	scissors	rock	candy bar
5		2	3	4					
6									

Figure 47: The formula pasted two rows down has arguments that are also shifted down two rows

One important point evident here is that the inconsistent formula does not affect the value outcome until cell C3! This is critical to understand because, sometimes, if you do not check your formula, you will think you are copying and pasting correctly – you may even spot-check a few cells that look right without even realizing the flaw.

I speak from very personal experience on this. It is unpleasant to work hard on a report that fails to provide the information expected. It is also not good for building credibility and trust with superiors and colleagues on the quality of your work.

Introducing the Dollar Sign

When designating a value as absolute, a dollar sign ($) is used. When the dollar sign is omitted, the reference will shift as the formula is copied and pasted into other cells. This segment will help you understand when and why to use the $, and soon you will understand the flexibility it provides.

As stated earlier, using a dollar sign before referencing a cell's column or row will make that reference absolute (or unchanged). The $ symbol informs Excel that we do not want the reference shifting as we paste the formula into different cells. By adding a $, that reference will not change.

Note that a column, a row, or both column and row can be referenced as either relative or absolute. That means that in one reference, we can keep a row the same (absolute), while the column changes (relative) as we copy and paste from cell to cell.

Now, in cell B2, type the following:

=VLOOKUP($A2,$F$1:$I$4,B$5,0)

Do you see what's happening there?

In the lookup value argument, A is absolute, while 2 is relative

In the table array argument, both F and 1, as well as I and 4, are absolute

In the column index argument, B is relative, while 5 is absolute

When we copy and paste the formula from cell B2 into cells B2 through D4, the values will match G2 through I4. So, how did we do it?

First, we kept the lookup value's column A absolute so it always refers back to column A on any row or column.

	A	B	C	D	E	F	G	H	I
1	Lookup Value	Item 1	Item 2	Item 3		Lookup Value	Item 1	Item 2	Item 3
2	Ref1	=VLOOKUP($A2,$F$1:$I$4,B$5,0)				Ref1	rock	paper	scissors
3	Ref2	rock	scissors	chicken nuggets		Ref2	rock	scissors	chicken nuggets
4	Ref3	scissors	rock	candy bar		Ref3	scissors	rock	candy bar
5		2	3	4					

Figure 48: An absolute reference to column A

Then, we kept the lookup value's row 2 relative, so it will change as we travel down the table. See cell C3 as a clear demonstration of this.

	A	B	C	D	E	F	G	H	I
1	Lookup Value	Item 1	Item 2	Item 3		Lookup Value	Item 1	Item 2	Item 3
2	Ref1	rock	paper	scissors		Ref1	rock	paper	scissors
3	Ref2	rock	=VLOOKUP($A3,$F$1:$I$4,C$5,0)				rock	scissors	chicken nuggets
4	Ref3	scissors	rock	candy bar		Ref3	scissors	rock	candy bar
5		2	3	4					

Figure 49: An absolute column and relative cell lookup value maintains an effective formula wherever it's placed

Both the columns and rows of the table array are absolute, so they will remain constant throughout.

Finally, the column index uses a relative column and an absolute row. Cell B2 has B$5 as the column index. When this is copied, its row will stay the same but the column will shift, as shown in the preceding illustration.

In row 5, cells B through D, we have a footer reference. In a VLOOKUP formula, when we use a literal number as a column index, that value stays the same. But when we use a relative reference, the number will shift as the formula is copied to other columns. By utilizing a footer with a reference as the column index, we won't have to manually adjust this argument in every cell we paste the formula.

Note that while our lookup value has an absolute column reference and a relative row, the column index has the converse – a relative column and an absolute row.

This was a lot to tackle, and we are going to look at a familiar example for another approach at getting our heads wrapped around absolute and relative references.

Multiplication Table

Consider this old multiplication table from elementary school, available in the worksheet named Multiplication Tables.

	A	B	C	D	E	F	G	H	I	J	K	L
1	1	2	3	4	5	6	7	8	9	10	11	12
2	2	4	6	8	10	12	14	16	18	20	22	24
3	3	6	9	12	15	18	21	24	27	30	33	36
4	4	8	12	16	20	24	28	32	36	40	44	48
5	5	10	15	20	25	30	35	40	45	50	55	60
6	6	12	18	24	30	36	42	48	54	60	66	72
7	7	14	21	28	35	42	49	56	63	70	77	84
8	8	16	24	32	40	48	56	64	72	80	88	96
9	9	18	27	36	45	54	63	72	81	90	99	108
10	10	20	30	40	50	60	70	80	90	100	110	120
11	11	22	33	44	55	66	77	88	99	110	121	132
12	12	24	36	48	60	72	84	96	108	120	132	144

Figure 50: The multiplication table with the working area bordered in black

We will attempt to duplicate cells B2 through L12 using VLOOKUP. This will help better explain how the relative and absolute references are interacting as we traverse from cell to cell.

We will use the first column of our multiplication table as the lookup value, the entire table as the table array, and the first row as the column index.

If we enter the following into cell N2, it should display the value 4:

=VLOOKUP(A2,A1:L12,B1,0)

When we copy the formula in N2, select N2 through X12, and then paste, we can see where our formula went wrong. Cell O2 should have a 6, but it shows an 8. This is the result of a relative lookup value that has shifted to cell B2 (with a value of 4).

	N	O	P	Q	R	S	T	U	V	W	X
1											
2	4	8	12	16	20	24	4	12	20	4	20
3	12	21	30	0	30	#REF!	#REF!	#REF!	#REF!	#REF!	#REF!
4	24	40	24	#REF!	#REF!	#REF!	#REF!	#REF!	#REF!	#REF!	#REF!
5	40	0	#REF!	#REF!	#REF!	#REF!	#REF!	#REF!	#REF!	#REF!	#REF!
6	60	#REF!	#REF!	#REF!	#REF!	#REF!	#REF!	#REF!	#REF!	#REF!	#REF!
7	84	#REF!	#REF!	#REF!	#REF!	#REF!	#REF!	#REF!	#REF!	#REF!	#REF!
8	#REF!	#REF!	#REF!	#REF!	#REF!	#REF!	#REF!	#REF!	#REF!	#REF!	#REF!
9	#REF!	#REF!	#REF!	#REF!	#REF!	#REF!	#REF!	#REF!	#REF!	#REF!	#REF!
10	#REF!	#REF!	#REF!	#REF!	#REF!	#REF!	#REF!	#REF!	#REF!	#REF!	#REF!
11	#REF!	#REF!	#REF!	#REF!	#REF!	#REF!	#REF!	#REF!	#REF!	#REF!	#REF!
12	#REF!	#REF!	#REF!	#REF!	#REF!	#REF!	#REF!	#REF!	#REF!	#REF!	#REF!

Figure 51: With a relative lookup value, the formula goes awry in a new location

If we adjust the formula in cell N2 to make the lookup value absolute...

=VLOOKUP($A2,A1:L12,B1,0)

we can once again copy N2 and paste the formula over cells N2 through X12. And, once again, we see errors in the cells; however, they are different from the errors shown earlier.

If we check the formula in cell O2, we now see 4 instead of 6. Now, the table array is still relative, so our lookup value is 2. But the table array has shifted to start in column B, where the number 2 appears in row 1.

Then, based on the column index, Excel moves over three cells to the right and finds the value 4. The logic only gets messier as we look at the formula in other cells.

	N	O	P	Q	R	S	T	U	V	W	X
1											
2	4	4	#N/A	#N/A	#N/A	#N/A	#N/A	#N/A	#N/A	#N/A	#N/A
3	12	#N/A	#N/A	#N/A	#N/A	#N/A	#N/A	#N/A	#N/A	#N/A	#N/A
4	24	#N/A	#N/A	#N/A	#N/A	#N/A	#N/A	#N/A	#N/A	#N/A	#N/A
5	40	#N/A	#N/A	#N/A	#N/A	#N/A	#N/A	#N/A	#N/A	#N/A	#N/A
6	60	#N/A	#N/A	#N/A	#N/A	#N/A	#N/A	#N/A	#N/A	#N/A	#N/A
7	84	#N/A	#N/A	#N/A	#N/A	#N/A	#N/A	#N/A	#N/A	#N/A	#N/A
8	#REF!	#N/A	#N/A	#N/A	#N/A	#N/A	#N/A	#N/A	#N/A	#N/A	#N/A
9	#REF!	#N/A	#N/A	#N/A	#N/A	#N/A	#N/A	#N/A	#N/A	#N/A	#N/A
10	#REF!	#N/A	#N/A	#N/A	#N/A	#N/A	#N/A	#N/A	#N/A	#N/A	#N/A
11	#REF!	#N/A	#N/A	#N/A	#N/A	#N/A	#N/A	#N/A	#N/A	#N/A	#N/A
12	#REF!	#N/A	#N/A	#N/A	#N/A	#N/A	#N/A	#N/A	#N/A	#N/A	#N/A

Figure 52: The problem is not corrected by merely adding an absolute column to the lookup value

So, we will need to rewrite the formula in N2 to make sure both the columns and rows are absolute, to keep the table array constant regardless of where it is referenced:

=VLOOKUP($A2,$A$1:$L$12,B1,0)

Again, copy cell N2 and paste over the earlier values in cells N2 through X12.

	N	O	P	Q	R	S	T	U	V	W	X
1											
2	4	6	8	10	12	14	16	18	20	22	24
3	12	18	24	30	36	#REF!	#REF!	#REF!	#REF!	#REF!	#REF!
4	24	36	48	#REF!	#REF!	#REF!	#REF!	#REF!	#REF!	#REF!	#REF!
5	40	60	#REF!	#REF!	#REF!	#REF!	#REF!	#REF!	#REF!	#REF!	#REF!
6	60	#REF!	#REF!	#REF!	#REF!	#REF!	#REF!	#REF!	#REF!	#REF!	#REF!
7	84	#REF!	#REF!	#REF!	#REF!	#REF!	#REF!	#REF!	#REF!	#REF!	#REF!
8	#REF!	#REF!	#REF!	#REF!	#REF!	#REF!	#REF!	#REF!	#REF!	#REF!	#REF!
9	#REF!	#REF!	#REF!	#REF!	#REF!	#REF!	#REF!	#REF!	#REF!	#REF!	#REF!
10	#REF!	#REF!	#REF!	#REF!	#REF!	#REF!	#REF!	#REF!	#REF!	#REF!	#REF!
11	#REF!	#REF!	#REF!	#REF!	#REF!	#REF!	#REF!	#REF!	#REF!	#REF!	#REF!
12	#REF!	#REF!	#REF!	#REF!	#REF!	#REF!	#REF!	#REF!	#REF!	#REF!	#REF!

Figure 53: Making the columns and rows of the table array absolute doesn't entirely fix the problem, either

Row 1 of the table looks correct, and if you need to confirm, remember your twos multiplication table.

But row 2 of the table does not make any sense, and based on the reference errors, we can see we need to revise this formula further. Check the formula in cell N3 and you will notice that our column index is not pointing to row 1. We need to adjust the formula to make the row of the column index absolute.

Notice that we do not want to make the column absolute, or we'll see column B repeated eleven times in N2 through X12. The following formula is correct:

=VLOOKUP($A2,$A$1:$L$12,B$1,0)

This formula should replicate the multiplication table from 2 through 12.

PROJECT – REGISTRATION FORM

The goal of this project is create a registration form, to insert and store data's as name, address and phone. There are thousands of ways to create this form, on this project, will need to create a form that interacts with Excel worksheet. The form will read, insert and delete data's from worksheet.

The following picture shows the form model of this project.

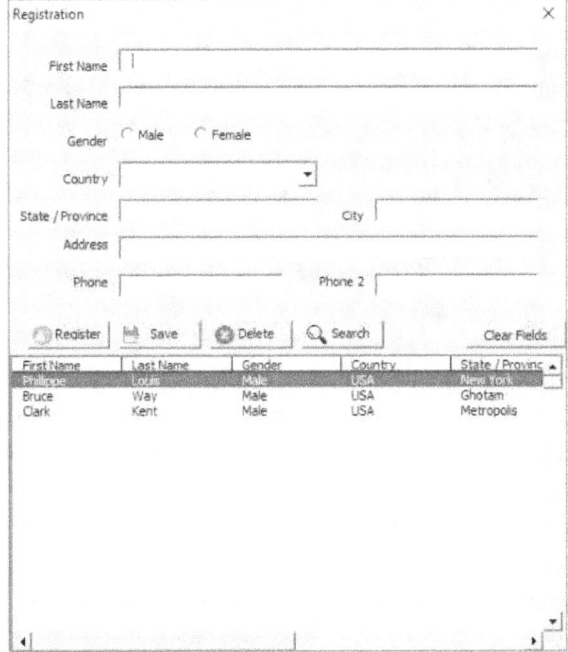

The Search Button open a new form as the following picture:

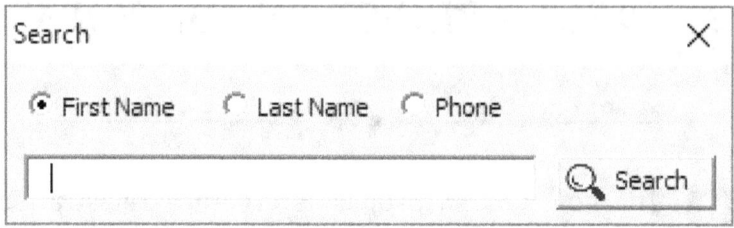

The worksheet will work as a database for the registration information, as the following picture:

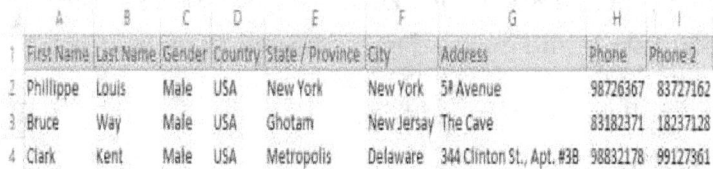

The buttons objects do the following functionalities:

Register – Add a new register at the end of the list

Save – Save modifications

Delete – Delete the existing registration

Search – Open the search form, that find a registration

Clear Fields – Clear all text boxes information's

Solution registration form:

Public NAME, LNAME, GENDER, COUNTRY, STATE, CITY, ADDRESS, PHONE, PHONE2 As String

```vba
Public nRow As Long

Public pos As Long

Public ChangesOK As Boolean

    Private Sub UserForm_Initialize()

        ChangesOK = True

    End Sub

Private Sub BT_REGISTER_Click()

    nRow = Application.WorksheetFunction.CountA(Range("A:A")) + 1

    Call UpdateText

    If NAME = "" Or COUNTRY = "" Or ADDRESS = "" Then

        MsgBox ("Incomplete Form")

    Else

    Call Insert

    End If

End Sub

Private Sub BT_SAVE_Click()

    ChangesOK = False
```

```
pos = LB_REGISTERS.ListIndex + 2

Range("A" & pos) = TXT_NAME.Value

Range("B" & pos) = TXT_LNAME.Value

If OB_MALE.Value = True = True Then

    Range("C" & pos) = "Male"

Else

    Range("C" & pos) = "Female"

End If

    Range("D" & pos) = CB_COUNTRY.Value

    Range("E" & pos) = TXT_STATE.Value

    Range("F" & pos) = TXT_CITY.Value

    Range("G" & pos) = TXT_ADDRESS.Value

    Range("H" & pos) = TXT_PHONE.Value

    Range("I" & pos) = TXT_PHONE2.Value

    ChangesOK = True

End Sub

Private Sub BT_DELETE_Click()

    pos = LB_REGISTERS.ListIndex + 2

    Rows(pos).Delete
```

```
        On Error Resume Next

            LB_REGISTERS.Selected(pos - 1) = True
End Sub

Private Sub BT_SEARCH_Click()

        FORM_SEARCH.Show

End Sub

Private Sub BT_CLEAR_Click()

        TXT_NAME.Value = ""

        TXT_LNAME.Value = ""

        OB_MALE.Value = True

        CB_COUNTRY.Value = ""

        TXT_STATE.Value = ""

        TXT_CITY.Value = ""

        TXT_ADDRESS.Value = ""

        TXT_PHONE.Value = ""

        TXT_PHONE2.Value = ""

End Sub

Private Sub LB_REGISTERS_Change()

If ChangesOK = False Then
```

        Exit Sub

End If

TXT_NAME.Value = LB_REGISTERS.List(LB_REGISTERS.ListIndex, 0)

TXT_LNAME.Value = LB_REGISTERS.List(LB_REGISTERS.ListIndex, 1)

If LB_REGISTERS.List(LB_REGISTERS.ListIndex, 2) = "Male" Then

        OB_MALE.Value = True

        OB_FEMALE.Value = False

Else

        OB_MALE.Value = False

        OB_FEMALE.Value = True

End If

CB_COUNTRY.Value = LB_REGISTERS.List(LB_REGISTERS.ListIndex, 3)

TXT_STATE.Value = LB_REGISTERS.List(LB_REGISTERS.ListIndex, 4)

TXT_CITY.Value = LB_REGISTERS.List(LB_REGISTERS.ListIndex, 5)

TXT_ADDRESS.Value = LB_REGISTERS.List(LB_REGISTERS.ListIndex, 6)

```
TXT_PHONE.Value = LB_REGISTERS.List(LB_REGISTERS.ListIndex, 7)

TXT_PHONE2.Value = LB_REGISTERS.List(LB_REGISTERS.ListIndex, 8)

End Sub

Public Sub Insert()

        Range("A" & nRow) = NAME

        Range("B" & nRow) = LNAME

        Range("C" & nRow) = GENDER

        Range("D" & nRow) = COUNTRY

        Range("E" & nRow) = STATE

        Range("F" & nRow) = CITY

        Range("G" & nRow) = ADDRESS

        Range("H" & nRow) = PHONE

        Range("I" & nRow) = PHONE2

End Sub

Public Sub UpdateText()

        NAME = TXT_NAME.Value

        LNAME = TXT_LNAME.Value

If OB_MALE.Value = True Then
```

```
            GENDER = "Male"
    Else
            GENDER = "Female"
    End If
            COUNTRY = CB_COUNTRY.Value
            STATE = TXT_STATE.Value
            CITY = TXT_CITY.Value
            ADDRESS = TXT_ADDRESS.Value
            PHONE = TXT_PHONE.Value
            PHONE2 = TXT_PHONE2.Value
    End Sub
```

Solution search form:

```
Private Sub BT_SEARCH_Click()
Dim COL As String
Dim ROW As String
Dim TXTSEARCH As String
If OB_SNAME.Value = True Then
        COL = "A"
ElseIf OB_SLNAME.Value = True Then
```

```
        COL = "B"
ElseIf OB_SPHONE.Value = True Then
        COL = "H"
End If
        TXTSEARCH = TXT_SEARCH
On Error GoTo sError
If IsNumeric(TXTSEARCH) Then
        ROW = Application.WorksheetFunction.Match(CLng(TXTSEARCH), Range(COL & ":" & COL), 0)
Else
        ROW = Application.WorksheetFunction.Match(CStr(TXTSEARCH), Range(COL & ":" & COL), 0)
End If
        FORM_REGISTER.LB_REGISTERS.Selected(ROW - 2) = True
Exit Sub
sError:
        MsgBox "Registration not found"
End Sub
```

```
Private Sub TXT_SEARCH_KeyDown(ByVal KeyCode As
MSForms.ReturnInteger, ByVal Shift As Integer)

    If KeyCode = 13 Then

        Call BT_SEARCH_Click

    End If

End Sub
```

Explanation registration form:

The first step of this project is declare the variables, there many subs, then the variables are declared in a public way. The strings just represent the values of text boxes. The nRow and pos are used to count position and ChangesOK is a Boolean that will work as a trick that avoid the Sub LB_REGISTERS_Change() when necessary.

Public NAME, LNAME, GENDER, COUNTRY, STATE, CITY, ADDRESS, PHONE, PHONE2 As String

Public nRow, pos As Long

Public ChangesOK As Boolean

After define the project variables, is necessary create the sub instructions. There are nine Sub's in the Registration form, each one is fundamental for the application functionality.

The Main Form:

UserForm_Initialize()

BT_REGISTER_Click()

BT_SAVE_Click()

BT_DELETE_Click()

BT_SEARCH_Click()

BT_CLEAR_Click()

LB_REGISTERS_Change()

Insert()

UpdateText()

The Search Form:

BT_SEARCH_Click()

TXT_SEARCH_KeyDown()

The following diagram, explain how the Subs are connected:

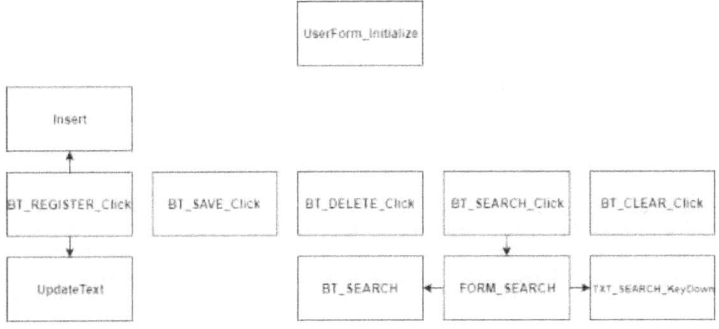

The Main Form explanation:

UserForm_Initialize()

This sub activate when the form starts, it's used just to define the Boolean ChangesOK with false value.

BT_REGISTER_Click()

First Step

Set the variable nRow to get the total of used rows, using the method Application.WorksheetFunction.CountA.

Second Step

Call the "UpdateText" Sub, which associate the variables with Text Boxes values, then the" if Statement", verifies if three important variables are empty or not.

Third Step

Call the "Insert" Sub, which fill the cells with variable values.

BT_SAVE_Click()

First Step

Set the Boolean ChangesOK as False, it is necessary to avoid the sub LB_REGISTERS_Change() in this case.

Second Step

Set the variable "pos" as LB_REGISTERS.ListIndex + 2, this variable represent the row position in the worksheet, it is necessary sum 2 because the ListBox count from zero while the worksheet row start with 1 and the worksheet also has a head.

Third Step

The last Step of this Sub is set the Cells values to get the Forms information. There are a "if statement" to check if ComboBox is with male of female value.

Range("A" & pos) = TXT_NAME.Value

Range("B" & pos) = TXT_LNAME.Value

    If OB_MALE.Value = True = True Then

        Range("C" & pos) = "Male"

    Else

        Range("C" & pos) = "Female"

    End If

Range("D" & pos) = CB_COUNTRY.Value

Range("E" & pos) = TXT_STATE.Value

Range("F" & pos) = TXT_CITY.Value

Range("G" & pos) = TXT_ADDRESS.Value

Range("H" & pos) = TXT_PHONE.Value

Range("I" & pos) = TXT_PHONE2.Value

BT_DELETE_Click()

First Step

Set the variable pos as LB_REGISTERS.ListIndex + 2, this variable represent the row position in the worksheet, it is necessary sum 2 because the ListBox count from zero while the worksheet row start with 1 and the worksheet also has a head.

Second Step

The second step is just for delete the row with Rows(pos).Delete

Third Step

The last step of this sub select the ListBox item earlier. The "On Error Resume Next" is applied to prevent error if the user delete the first row.

On Error Resume Next

    LB_REGISTERS.Selected(pos - 1) = True

    BT_SEARCH_Click()

This sub is just to show the Search Form.

    FORM_SEARCH.Show

    BT_CLEAR_Click()

This sub is just to clear all fields and select the default Option Button as Male. The procedure to clear fields is simple, just set the value as empty using "".

    TXT_NAME.Value = ""

```
TXT_LNAME.Value = ""

OB_MALE.Value = True

CB_COUNTRY.Value = ""

TXT_STATE.Value = ""

TXT_CITY.Value = ""

TXT_ADDRESS.Value = ""

TXT_PHONE.Value = ""

TXT_PHONE2.Value = ""
```

LB_REGISTERS_Change()

This sub is activated for any selection change inside the list. It provides the update of the forms fields with ListBox selection.

First Step

As mentioned the ChangesOK Boolean works as a trick to run the update just when necessary. When the Boolean is false, the code exit the Sub.

```
If ChangesOK = False Then

    Exit Sub
```

Second Step

Each Text Box and the Option Button (Male and Female) are updated according to the ListBox selection. The following code do this procedure. For the option box, the "If Statement" provides the correct selection according to the ListBox information (Male or Female).

TXT_NAME.Value = LB_REGISTERS.List(LB_REGISTERS.ListIndex, 0)

TXT_LNAME.Value = LB_REGISTERS.List(LB_REGISTERS.ListIndex, 1)

If LB_REGISTERS.List(LB_REGISTERS.ListIndex, 2) = "Male" Then

    OB_MALE.Value = True

    OB_FEMALE.Value = False

Else

    OB_MALE.Value = False

    OB_FEMALE.Value = True

End If

CB_COUNTRY.Value = LB_REGISTERS.List(LB_REGISTERS.ListIndex, 3)

TXT_STATE.Value = LB_REGISTERS.List(LB_REGISTERS.ListIndex, 4)

TXT_CITY.Value = LB_REGISTERS.List(LB_REGISTERS.ListIndex, 5)

TXT_ADDRESS.Value = LB_REGISTERS.List(LB_REGISTERS.ListIndex, 6)

TXT_PHONE.Value = LB_REGISTERS.List(LB_REGISTERS.ListIndex, 7)

TXT_PHONE2.Value = LB_REGISTERS.List(LB_REGISTERS.ListIndex, 8)

Insert()

As mentioned, this sub will just update the worksheet information according to the Variables values.

Range("A" & nRow) = NAME

Range("B" & nRow) = LNAME

Range("C" & nRow) = GENDER

Range("D" & nRow) = COUNTRY

Range("E" & nRow) = STATE

Range("F" & nRow) = CITY

Range("G" & nRow) = ADDRESS

Range("H" & nRow) = PHONE

Range("I" & nRow) = PHONE2

UpdateText()

As mentioned, this sub will just update the variables according with Text Box and Option Button information. The Option Button, uses a "if Statement" to associate the gender.

NAME = TXT_NAME.Value

LNAME = TXT_LNAME.Value

    If OB_MALE.Value = True Then

        GENDER = "Male"

    Else

        GENDER = "Female"

    End If

COUNTRY = CB_COUNTRY.Value

STATE = TXT_STATE.Value

CITY = TXT_CITY.Value

ADDRESS = TXT_ADDRESS.Value

PHONE = TXT_PHONE.Value

PHONE2 = TXT_PHONE2.Value

The Search Form explanation:

BT_SEARCH_Click()

The Search form has just two subs, the first is the Search Button, and it use the option box to find a name, a last name or the phone number in the ListBox. The second sub is just to recognize the Enter button to activate the Search Button.

First Step

The first step is the variable declarations, there are three variables declared as Strings that will receive the column position ("COL"), the row position ("ROW") and the text to find ("TXTSEARCH").

Dim COL As String

Dim ROW As String

Dim TXTSEARCH As String

Second Step

The second step verifies the selected Option Box to define the column. The variable TXTSEARCH get the textbox value.

If OB_SNAME.Value = True Then

    COL = "A"

ElseIf OB_SLNAME.Value = True Then

    COL = "B"

ElseIf OB_SPHONE.Value = True Then

    COL = "H"

End If

TXTSEARCH = TXT_SEARCH

Third Step

The "On Error GoTo sError" works moving the code reading to the end with sError label. Then an MsgBox display the message: "Registration not found".

Fourth Step

The last step verifies if the TXTSEARCH is a number or not, then the "Application.WorkSheetFunction.Match", return the row, the method Selected with True Value activates the searched line in the listbox. The ROW is subtracting 2 for the difference between the worksheet and the listbox, the sheet start counting from 1 and it has a header, while the listbox starts from zero.

If IsNumeric(TXTSEARCH) Then

>ROW=Application.WorksheetFunction.Match(CLng(TXTSEARCH), Range(COL & ":" & COL), 0)

Else

>ROW=Application.WorksheetFunction.Match(CStr(TXTSEARCH), Range(COL & ":" & COL), 0)

End If

>FORM_REGISTER.LB_REGISTERS.Selected(ROW - 2) = True

Exit Sub

TXT_SEARCH_KeyDown()

This sub works just to recognize the Enter Button that will call the "BT_SEARCH_Click", the "if statement" is verifying if the user pressed the Enter Key, that KeyCode is 13.

```
Private Sub TXT_SEARCH_KeyDown(ByVal KeyCode As MSForms.ReturnInteger, ByVal Shift As Integer)

    If KeyCode = 13 Then

        Call BT_SEARCH_Click

    End If
```

A SAMPLE PROGRAM

We will go through a sample program that adopts most of the mentioned ideas with the following characteristics:

When the workbook is opened,

- A particular worksheet (named Sample) is activated.
- The first three rows are frozen.
- A particular row (row 50) is scrolled up and becomes the top row in the unfrozen pane.
- The scroll area for the active sheet is limited to certain range (A4:H100).
- A custom tab (named Custom) is activated.
- A drop-down control is dynamically filled with items (which are labelled as: All Groups, Group 1, Group 2, Group 3, Groups 1 and 2, Groups 1 and 3, and Groups 2 and 3) at runtime.
- A gallery control is dynamically filled with images at runtime.

When the user selects a different item from the drop-down control on the Custom tab,

- Only certain groups of controls on the tab (either all groups, Group 1, Group 2, Group 3, Groups 1 and 2,

Groups 1 and 3, or Groups 2 and 3) are displayed accordingly.
- The status bar displays the currently selected item.
- If a particular item (namely, Group 2) is selected, a particular worksheet (named Sheet2) is then activated with the following changes to its appearance:
  - ➤ The worksheet is displayed in page layout view.
  - ➤ The row and column headings are hidden.
  - ➤ The gridlines in the worksheet are removed.
  - ➤ The formula bar is hidden.

The Custom tab is visible if the activated sheet is a worksheet.

A custom control (namely, the G5B1 button on the View tab) is disabled (or enabled) if a particular built-in checkbox (namely, the Formula Bar check box on the View tab) is unticked (or ticked).

A set of control buttons in different groups on the Custom tab (namely: G1B1 in Group 1, G2B2 in Group 2, G3B3 in Group 3, and G4B3 in Group 4) is enabled if the activated worksheet (named Sheet1) has a particular worksheet-level named range (namely, a range named MyRange). Otherwise, the set of buttons is disabled.

A custom control (named Remove USD) can be accessed from the Cell context menu

To build the program, execute the following steps:

1. Create a new workbook and save it as a macro-enabled workbook.
2. Right-click a sheet tab and choose Insert to add a chart sheet.
3. Add additional worksheets if needed and rename a worksheet Sample, a worksheet Sheet1, and another worksheet Sheet2.
4. Activate the Sheet1 worksheet, select a range of cells, and in the Name box enter Sheet1!MyRange to name the range a worksheet-level name of MyRange.
5. If the Name box is not visible, tick the Formula Bar check box on the View tab.
6. Close the workbook and open it in Custom UI Editor.
7. In Custom UI Editor, click Insert and choose Office 2010 Custom UI Part.

Copy and paste the following XML code:

<customUI

xmlns="http://schemas.microsoft.com/office/2009/07/customui"

onLoad="Initialize">

<commands>

<command idMso="ViewFormulaBar"

　　　onAction="MonitorViewFormulaBar"/>

</commands>

```xml
<ribbon>
<tabs>
<tab id="CustomTab" label="Custom"
    insertBeforeMso="TabView"
    getVisible="getVisibleCustomTab">
<group id="GroupGallerye" label="Gallery" >
<gallery id="gallery1"
    label="Photos"
    imageMso="Camera"
    size="large"
    itemWidth="100"
    itemHeight="100"
    onAction="SelectedPhoto"
    getItemCount="getGalleryItemCount"
    getItemImage="getGalleryItemImage"/>
</group>
<group id="GroupModule" label="Modules" >
<dropDown id="dropDown1"
    label="Module:"
```

```
            sizeString="xxxxxxxxxxxxxxxxxx"

            onAction="SelectedItem"

            getItemCount="getDropDownItemCount"

            getItemLabel="getDropDownItemLabel">
</dropDown>
</group>
<group id="Group1" label="Group 1"
            getVisible="getVisibleGrp">
<button id="G1B1" label="G1B1" imageMso="Copy"
            onAction="MacroG1B1"
            getEnabled="getEnabledBs"/>
</group>
<group id="Group2" label="Group 2"
            getVisible="getVisibleGrp" >
<button id="G2B1" label="G2B1" imageMso="Bold"onAction="MacroG2B1" />

<button id="G2B2" label="G2B2" imageMso="Italic" onAction="MacroG2B2" getEnabled="getEnabledBs"/>
</group>
<group id="Group3" label="Group 3"getVisible="getVisibleGrp" >
```

```xml
<button id="G3B1" label="G3B1" imageMso="_1" onAction="MacroG3B1" />

<button id="G3B2" label="G3B2" imageMso="_2" onAction="MacroG3B2" />

<button id="G3B3" label="G3B3" imageMso="_3" onAction="MacroG3B3" getEnabled="getEnabledBs"/>

        </group>

        <group id="Group4" label="Group 4" >

<button id="G4B1" label="G4B1" imageMso="A" onAction="MacroG4B1" />

<button id="G4B2" label="G4B2" imageMso="B" onAction="MacroG4B2" />

<button id="G4B3" label="G4B3" imageMso="C" onAction="MacroG4B3" getEnabled="getEnabledBs"/>

</group>

</tab>

<tab idMso="TabView" >

<group id="Group5" label="Group 5"

        insertAfterMso="GroupViewShowHide">

<button id="G5B1" label="G5B1" imageMso="Camera"

        size="large" onAction="MacroG5B1"

        getEnabled="getEnabledG5B1"/>
```

```
</group>
</tab>
</tabs>
</ribbon>
<contextMenus>
<contextMenu idMso="ContextMenuCell">
<button id="RemoveUSD"
    label="Remove USD"
    insertBeforeMso="Cut"
    onAction="RemoveUSD"
    imageMso="HappyFace"/>
</contextMenu>
</contextMenus>
</customUI>
```

8. Click the Validate button on the toolbar to check for errors.

9. Save and close the file.

10. Open the file in Excel.

11. Click OK to the error messages.

12. Press Alt+11 to activate VBE.

13. Insert a standard VBA module and copy and paste the following VBA code into the module:

```vba
Public myRibbon As IRibbonUI

Dim ImageCount As Long   'Number of images in the gallery

Dim ImageFilenames() As String   'Filenames of the images

Dim ItemLabels(0 To 6) As String 'Item labels for the drop-down

Dim VisGrpNm1 As String 'Store the names of groups to be visible

Dim VisGrpNm2 As String 'when an item from the drop-down is selected

'Callback for customUI.onLoad

Sub Initialize(ribbon As IRibbonUI)

Set myRibbon = ribbon

'Activate the Custom tab

myRibbon.ActivateTab "CustomTab"

'Do not place the above line of code in Workbook_Open

'because myRibbon is still Nothing

'Prepare the filenames of the images for the gallery

Call PrepareItemImages
```

```
'Prepare the labels of the items for the drop-down

Call PrepareItemLabels

End Sub

Private Sub PrepareItemImages()

'To build an array of filenames of the images for the gallery

Dim Filename As String

Filename = Dir("C:\Photos\*.jpg")

'To loop through all the jpg files in the folder and populate

'the ImageFilenames array with the filenames of the jpg files

Do While Filename <> ""

ImageCount = ImageCount + 1

ReDim Preserve ImageFilenames(1 To ImageCount)

ImageFilenames(ImageCount) = Filename

    Filename = Dir

    Loop

    'Dir() returns a zero-length string ("")

    'when no more file in the folder matches
```

'the pathname, "C:\Photos*.jpg"

End Sub

'Callback for gallery1 getItemCount

Sub getGalleryItemCount(control As IRibbonControl, ByRef Count)

'To specify the number of times to call

'the getGalleryItemImage procedure

    Count = ImageCount

End Sub

'Callback for gallery1 getItemImage

Sub getGalleryItemImage(control As IRibbonControl, _

    index As Integer, ByRef Image)

'Each time this procedure is called, index is increased by one

Set Image = LoadPicture("C:\Photos\" & ImageFilenames(index + 1))

End Sub

'Callback for gallery1 onAction

Sub SelectedPhoto(control As IRibbonControl, id As String, index As Integer)

    MsgBox "You selected Photo " & index + 1

End Sub

Private Sub PrepareItemLabels()

'To build an array of item labels for the drop-down

    Dim i As Long

    ItemLabels(0) = "All Groups"

    ItemLabels(1) = "Group 1"

    ItemLabels(2) = "Group 2"

    ItemLabels(3) = "Group 3"

    ItemLabels(4) = "Groups 1 and 2"

    ItemLabels(5) = "Groups 1 and 3"

    ItemLabels(6) = "Groups 2 and 3"

End Sub

'Callback for dropDown1 getItemCount

Sub getDropDownItemCount(control As IRibbonControl, ByRef Count)

'To specify the total number of items in the drop-down control

    Count = 7

End Sub

'Callback for dropDown1 getItemLabel

```
Sub getDropDownItemLabel(control As IribbonControl, index As Integer, ByRef ItemLabel)
'Set the item labels in the drop-down control
    ItemLabel = ItemLabels(index)
'Alternatively, if the item labels are in stored
'the range A1:A7 on Sheet1, use the following code:
'ItemLabel = Worksheets("Sheet1").Cells(index + 1, 1).Value
End Sub

'Callback for dropDown1 onAction
Sub SelectedItem(control As IRibbonControl, _
    id As String, index As Integer)
'Determine which group(s) to be visible
    VisGrpNm1 = "": VisGrpNm2 = ""
Select Case index
    Case 0
        VisGrpNm1 = "*"
    Case 1
        VisGrpNm1 = "*1"
    Case 2
```

```
            VisGrpNm1 = "*2"

    'Change the appearance of Sheet2 if 3rd item is selected

    Call ChangeSheet2Appearance

        Case 3

            VisGrpNm1 = "*3"

        Case 4

            VisGrpNm1 = "*1"

            VisGrpNm2 = "*2"

        Case 5

            VisGrpNm1 = "*1"

            VisGrpNm2 = "*3"

        Case 6

            VisGrpNm1 = "*2"

            VisGrpNm2 = "*3"

    End Select

    'Invalidate Group1, Group2, and Group3

    'Once invalidated, getVisibleGrp is executed

    myRibbon.InvalidateControl "Group1"

    myRibbon.InvalidateControl "Group2"
```

```vba
    myRibbon.InvalidateControl "Group3"
    'Update the status bar
    Application.StatusBar = " Module: " & ItemLabels(index)
End Sub

'Callback for Group1 getVisible
Sub getVisibleGrp(control As IRibbonControl, ByRef Enabled)
    'Hide and unhide certain groups of 1, 2, and 3
    'based on the selected item from the drop-down control
    If control.id Like VisGrpNm1 Or control.id Like VisGrpNm2 Then
            Enabled = True  'Visible
    Else
            Enabled = False 'Hidden
    End If
End Sub

Private Sub ChangeSheet2Appearance()
    Application.ScreenUpdating = False
    Sheets("Sheet2").Activate
    With ActiveWindow
```

'To display the active worksheet in page layout view

.View = xlPageLayoutView

'To hide the row and column headings

.DisplayHeadings = False

'To hide the gridlines

.DisplayGridlines = False

End With

'To hide the formula bar

  Application.DisplayFormulaBar = False

  Application.ScreenUpdating = True

End Sub

'Callback for G1B1, G2B2, G3B3, and G4B3 getEnabled

Sub getEnabledBs(control As IRibbonControl, ByRef Enabled)

'The set of G1B1, G2B2, G3B3, and G4B3 buttons is enabled

'if the active sheet has a range named MyRange

'In this program, this procedure is called when the Ribbon

'is invalidated in the Workbook_SheetActivate event handler

```vba
    Enabled = RngNameExists(ActiveSheet, "MyRange")

End Sub

Function RngNameExists(ws As Worksheet, RngName As String) As Boolean

'To return whether a named range exists in a worksheet

    Dim rng As Range

    On Error Resume Next

    Set rng = ws.Range(RngName)

    RngNameExists = Err.Number = 0

End Function

'Callback for ViewFormulaBar onAction

Sub MonitorViewFormulaBar(control As IRibbonControl, _
    pressed As Boolean, ByRef cancelDefault)

    cancelDefault = False  'Restore the functionality of the control

    myRibbon.InvalidateControl "G5B1"

End Sub

'Callback for G5B1 getEnabled

Sub getEnabledG5B1(control As IRibbonControl, ByRef Enabled)
```

'The GSB1 button is enabled if the formula bar is visible

Enabled = Application.DisplayFormulaBar

End Sub

'Callback for CustomTab getVisible

Sub getVisibleCustomTab(control As IRibbonControl, _

ByRef CustomTabVisible)

CustomTabVisible = TypeName(ActiveSheet) = "Worksheet"

End Sub

The Custom tab is visible if the active sheet is a worksheet. In this program, this procedure is called when the Ribbon is invalidated in the Workbook_SheetActivate event handler.

'Callback for G1B1 onAction

Sub MacroG1B1(control As IRibbonControl)

    MsgBox "MacroG1B1"

End Sub

'Callback for G2B1 onAction

Sub MacroG2B1(control As IRibbonControl)

    MsgBox "MacroG2B1"

End Sub

```vba
'Callback for G2B2 onAction
Sub MacroG2B2(control As IRibbonControl)
    MsgBox "MacroG2B2"
End Sub

'Callback for G3B1 onAction
Sub MacroG3B1(control As IRibbonControl)
    MsgBox "MacroG3B1"
End Sub

'Callback for G3B2 onAction
Sub MacroG3B2(control As IRibbonControl)
    MsgBox "MacroG3B2"
End Sub

'Callback for G3B3 onAction
Sub MacroG3B3(control As IRibbonControl)
    MsgBox "MacroG3B3"
End Sub

'Callback for G4B1 onAction
Sub MacroG4B1(control As IRibbonControl)
    MsgBox "MacroG4B1"
```

End Sub

'Callback for G4B2 onAction

Sub MacroG4B2(control As IRibbonControl)

    MsgBox "MacroG4B2"

End Sub

'Callback for G4B3 onAction

Sub MacroG4B3(control As IRibbonControl)

    MsgBox "MacroG4B3"

End Sub

'Callback for G5B1 onAction

Sub MacroG5B1(control As IRibbonControl)

    MsgBox "MacroG5B1"

End Sub

Sub RemoveUSD(control As IRibbonControl)

'To remove the currency symbols in a range of selected cells

'For example, USD 500.25 becomes 500.25

Dim workRng As Range

Dim Item As Range

On Error Resume Next

```
Set workRng = Intersect(Selection, _
Selection.Cells.SpecialCells.(xlCellTypeConstants, xlTextValues))
If Not workRng Is Nothing Then
    For Each Item In workRng
    If UCase(Left(Item, 3)) = "USD" Then.Item = Right(Item, Len(Item) - 3)
    Next Item
End If
End Sub
```

14. Insert the following VBA code into the ThisWorkbook module:

```
Private Sub Workbook_Open()
With Application
'Disable Workbook_SheetActivate because
'myRibbon is still Nothing
    .EnableEvents = False
    .ScreenUpdating = False
End With
'Activate a particular worksheet
```

```
Worksheets("Sample").Activate
'Freeze the first three rows
With ActiveWindow
        If .View = xlPageLayoutView Then _
            .View = xlNormalView
        .SplitRow = 3
        .SplitColumn = 0
        .FreezePanes = True
End With
'Set row 50 to be the top row in the unfrozen pane
        ActiveWindow.ScrollRow = 50
'A message for the user
With Range("A50")
        .Value = "Scroll up to see other info"
        .Font.Bold = True
        .Activate
End With
'Set the scroll area for the active sheet
ActiveSheet.ScrollArea = "A4:H100"  'Limit to the range A4:H100
```

With Application

    .EnableEvents = True

    .ScreenUpdating = True

End With

End Sub

Private Sub Workbook_SheetActivate(ByVal Sh As Object)

'To invalidate all controls

myRibbon.Invalidate

End Sub

15. Save, close, and reopen the workbook in Excel.

MORE EXAMPLES

Coloring maximum values

Sub MaxValueColoring()

Dim lMaxValue As Double, rng As Range, cell As Range

Cells.Interior.ColorIndex = 0

Set rng = Range("A1").CurrentRegion

lMaxValue = WorksheetFunction.Max(rng)

For Each cell In rng

    If cell.Value = lMaxValue Then cell.Interior.ColorIndex = 22

Next cell

End Sub

In this example, we have created a macro to color the cell having the maximum value.

Here I have declared one variable lMaxValue as type Double and two Range objects rng and cell. Then we have added entire cells interior color to none. Why we are specifying the interior color to none at the beginning is to reset the background color to none if you are again running the procedure with new value.

We initialize rng with the numbers. For that, we use the CurrentRegion property from A1 cell. Whatever values are there it will be assigned to the rng Object variable.

Then we initialize lMaxValue with the maximum value of the numbers. We use the worksheet function Max to find the maximum value.

Finally, we color the maximum value. We use a For Each Next Loop to loop through each cell in the range in rng object variable.

Points to Note: instead of ColorIndex number 22 (red), you can use any ColorIndex number.

Hide sheet

This macro will hide sheet1.

Sub HideSheet()

    Sheets("Sheet1").Visible = False

End Sub

You can also use index number of the sheet, Sheets(1).Visible = False, if you know the index number. One advantage of using the index number is if you change the sheet name to some other name still the program will hide the first sheet. This may be useful for hiding the information from the end user.

Department wise password

Here we have three departments HR, Admin, Finance and their data in sheet2. When the department gets the report, they should view only the data relating to them by entering the password given to them.

First, create an Excel sheet and enter the heading HR, Admin and Finance in A1, B1 and C1 cell of Sheet2. Fill the first four rows of each column with the data like this.

Then hide sheets sheet2 and sheet3. Now run this macro from a module.

Sub Hide_Sheet1()

Dim Dept As String

Dim InputPass As String

Dim Password(1 To 3) As String

Password(1) = "Recruite"

Password(2) = "Approval"

Password(3) = "Accounts"

Dept = InputBox("Please enter your department name")

InputPass = InputBox("Please enter the password")

If Dept = "HR" And InputPass = Password(1) Then

```
        Sheets(1).Range("A1:A4").Value =
        Sheets(2).Range("A1:A4").Value
```

End If

If Dept = "Admin" And InputPass = Password(2) Then

```
        Sheets(1).Range("A1:A4").Value =
        Sheets(2).Range("B1:B4").Value
```

End If

If Dept = "Finance" And InputPass = Password(3) Then

```
        Sheets(1).Range("A1:A4").Value =
        Sheets(2).Range("C1:C4").Value
```

End If

End Sub

This example is used to demonstrate how you can use VBA in various ways.

Changing Background colors

You can change the background color using Interior.ColorIndex Property. Here the number 5 denotes Blue 3 for Red, 4 for Green and 6 for Yellow. The ColorIndex property can generate up to 57 colors. You can see the full list from this link https://msdn.microsoft.com/en-us/library/cc296089(v=office.12).aspx.

Sub BackgoundColor()

Range("A1:C5").Interior.ColorIndex = 5 ' 5=Blue

End Sub

Change Font color and size

To change the font color and font size of a particular Range. Hereby specifying the Font's ColorIndex property, you can change the color of the cells from A1:A3. Also if you use the size property of the font, you can change the size of the font.

Sub FontColor()

    Range("A1:A3").Font.ColorIndex = 3 ' 3=Red

    Range("A1:A3").Font.Size = 15

End Sub

Rename and Delete Worksheet

Sub RenameDelete()

    Sheets.Add

    ActiveSheet.Name = "Temporary Sheet"

    Sheets("Temporary Sheet").Delete

End Sub

Create New Workbook, Add Data, Save And Close The Workbook

Sub SaveandClose()

Workbooks.Add

ActiveWorkbook.Sheets("Sheet1").Range("A1") = "Sample Data"

ActiveWorkbook.SaveAs "MyNewWorkbook.xls"

ActiveWorkbook.Close

End Sub

You can use Add method of a Workbooks object to add a new workbook. Then you can enter data in A1 cell and then use SaveAs to give a name and the close it.

It will save in the default folder; you can mention the full path as "c:\Temp\MyNewWorkbook.xls"

Insert And Delete Rows And Columns

Sub InsertandDelete()

Rows(6).Insert 'It will insert a row at 6 row

Rows(6).Delete 'it will delete the row 6

Columns("E").Insert 'it will insert the column at E

Columns("E").Delete 'it will delete the column E

End Sub

You can use Insert and Delete Properties of Rows to insert and delete rows. Also, you can use Insert and Delete Properties of Columns.

Row Height And Column Width

Sub HeightandWidth()

    Rows(12).RowHeight = 33

    Columns(5).ColumnWidth = 35

End Sub

You can increase and decrease the row height and column width with this macro.

CONCLUSION

Microsoft Excel is one of the commonly used and easy to access tools for beginners and professionals to do their daily tasks. Other than keeping records, it helps to run formulas, evaluating and sorting data and making reports. No one can deny its importance and efficiency when it comes to performance. An add-on of VBA of Excel and Macros makes it even better option for the beginners and professionals as well. It makes things streamed in the best form.

With the help of an additional language such as VBA, it is helpful to perform some complicated and bundle tasks with the help of Excel. The language is easy to understand and macros can be practiced commonly to increase the work efficiency. The built-in library helps to keep the record of frequently used macros that helps to sort the data and perform multiple tasks efficiently.

To get the best out of VBA Excel Macros, you need to learn the best of its skills that help you to be a competent professional in the field. Learning it for the beginners and non-programmers is not a difficult task at all. All you need is a little resource, practice and a good understanding of codes. Moreover, you should know the proper use and placement of these codes in the right place. Eventually, you can get some of the macros as resources and examples that help you to increase practice and develop more macros of the same nature.

Learning about Power BI is one of the best decisions you will ever make. Today it is virtually impossible not to interact with Microsoft Excel at some point in time, either at work or at home. To manage your personal expenditure and business finances, you need Excel at some point. Power BI takes things a notch higher.

Everything that you have been able to do in Excel in terms of reporting and handling data can now be performed on Power BI, but with a better user experience. For all its benefits, Excel has several constraints that have been addressed in Power BI with respect to managing data. Power BI makes your work easier, and your reports more presentable.

A lot of people struggle with Excel, given that they find it complex. Power BI attempts to smoothen some of these challenges by providing a platform that users can enjoy without it being too technical. You can share dashboards and reports easily on Power BI, something that has always been a challenge on Excel.

By sharing a dashboard, you can collaborate on a report with people in different teams, and in the process making sure that everyone who matters has a role to play in developing the report. This makes it an ideal platform for group work.

Compared to other platforms that you can use for data analysis and reporting, Power BI is affordable. While you must pay to enjoy certain services, you can access some of the basic features for free.

For your business reporting needs, you will find Power BI a useful application that can help you get a lot of work done. You can create beautiful visualizations that will help you in decision-making, and if you present this to an audience, they will also appreciate the work you have done.

www.ingramcontent.com/pod-product-compliance
Lightning Source LLC
Chambersburg PA
CBHW071353210526
45465CB00001B/77